NATIONAL COUNCIL FOR THE SOCIAL STUDIES BULLETIN NO. 65

Economic Education: Links to the Social Studies

S. Stowell Symmes, *Editor*

National Council for the Social Studies

The National Council for the Social Studies wishes to express its appreciation to the Joint Council on Economic Education for providing the financial support that made it possible to print this Bulletin for all Regular Members of NCSS.

Library of Congress Catalog Card Number: 81-82818

ISBN 0-87986-041-3

Table of Contents

FOREWORD

Economics dominates the news. With each feverish rise and fall of the interest rates, each nervous twitch of the stock market, each statistical stammer of the Gross National Product, our lives are being filled with economic dilemmas of increasing complexity. Nor is this state of affairs completely undesirable. As the distinguished historian Carl Becker pointed out: "Economic distress will teach [human beings], if anything can, that realities are less dangerous than fancies."

Thus, economic education demands our attention today; for, while education is not a panacea for all ills identified by economists from Adam Smith to David Stockman, it is the principal way of helping young people to understand the economic problems and potentialities facing our nation and other countries in the world.

That is why this new Bulletin, *Economic Education: Links to the Social Studies,* is so welcome. It is timely; it is necessary; it is useful. Particularly significant is the fact that the Bulletin focuses on the links between economic education and the social studies; and, in exploring such relationships, it demonstrates — once again — the importance of an interdisciplinary approach to education.

Authors in this Bulletin talk about the appropriateness of a marriage between economic education and social studies education. I will go a step further and agree with those who argue that economic education is an integral part of social studies education. If the goal of social studies is to prepare young people to be knowledgeable and capable participating citizens, economic education is vital.

How appropriate, then, that this Bulletin is published by the National Council for the Social Studies in conjunction with the Joint Council on Economic Education! The sharing of editorial and financial responsibilities for its publication is another example of the value of cooperation between professional associations.

On behalf of the National Council for the Social Studies, I wish to thank editor S. Stowell Symmes, the authors of the chapters, and the Joint Council on Economic Education for their work in preparing this valuable publication.

Theodore Kaltsounis, *President*
National Council for the Social Studies

ABOUT THE AUTHORS

WILLIAM BECKER is Associate Professor of Economics, Indiana University at Bloomington. He was Executive Director of the Minnesota Council on Economic Education, and for many years he directed a Center for Economic Education at the University of Minnesota. He served on the American Economic Association standing committee on economic education, has conducted research on various aspects of economic education, and is a referee for articles for several professional journals. His extensive publications include articles in the *American Economic Review, The Journal of Economic Education,* and *The Social Studies.*

KENNETH CARLSON is Associate Professor of Social Science Education at Rutgers, the State University of New Jersey. He has published articles in several journals, including *Social Education, Review of Educational Research, Urban, The Social Studies,* and the *Social Science Record.* He served on the Advisory Committee for the Book Review Section of *Social Education;* and at NCSS conventions, he has presented numerous papers on subjects such as censorship, values education, critical thinking, equalizing educational opportunity, and sexism. He has had a special interest in the work of the Rutgers Labor Education Center.

GEORGE L. FERSH is New England Regional Representative for the Joint Council on Economic Education. While a Professor of Social Studies at New York University, he was involved with establishing the JCEE; and prior to his retirement, he served for over twenty years as JCEE Associate Director. In that capacity, he was responsible for organizing State Affiliated Councils and he directed numerous curriculum projects, including those involving conservation education, personal economics, and awards for teaching excellence. A widely published author of textbooks, curriculum guides, and journal articles, he was also editor of the first NCSS Bulletin on the Problems Approach.

JUNE V. GILLIARD is Director of Curriculum for the Joint Council on Economic Education. Her assignments include coordinating the *Economics-Political Science Series* publications and the Economics for a Multicultural Society Project. She has worked as a social studies teacher and, prior to joining the Joint Council staff, was employed as a state social studies consultant for the North Carolina Department of Public Instruction. She is past-president of the Council of State Social Studies Specialists, and, more recently, has served on the Board of Directors of the National Council for the Social Studies and on the Citizenship/Social Studies Advisory Committee for the National Assessment of Educational Progress.

CAROLE L. HAHN is Associate Professor in the Division of Educational Studies at Emory University. She is co-author of the book *Wingspread Workbook for Educational Change Agents*. She has conducted research on the adoption of innovations in economics teaching, has directed National Science Foundation institutes in economics, and has published articles on eliminating sexism from social studies. Her extensive professional commitments include serving as chairperson of the NCSS Publications Board, the Committee on Sexism and Social Justice, and the Executive Board of CUFA. She has been a member of the NCSS Board of Directors and she is currently vice-president of the National Council for the Social Studies.

H. MICHAEL HARTOONIAN is the Supervisor of Social Studies Education for the Wisconsin Department of Public Instruction, Madison. He is a national authority on social studies education and curriculum design and has taught and lectured throughout the United States and Central America. He has served as a classroom teacher, university professor, and administrator, and has been a member of numerous education commissions. He is past-president of the State Council of Social Studies Specialists, and serves on the Executive Board of the Social Science Education Consortium.

JACK L. NELSON is Professor of Education in the Graduate School of Education at Rutgers University. His work with NCSS includes active participation in the founding of the College and University Faculty Assembly of the NCSS, membership on the Executive Board of *Social Education*, service as book review editor of *Social Education*, chairing of the Teacher Education Committee, and membership on the Editorial Board of *Theory and Research in Social Education*. His most recent books are *Secondary Social Studies: Instruction, Curriculum and Evaluation* (Prentice-Hall, 1980), co-authored with John U. Michaelis; and *International Human Rights* (Coleman, 1980), with Vera Green.

FRANCIS W. RUSHING is presently the Executive Director of the Georgia Council on Economic Education, and Chairperson and Professor, Department of Economics, Georgia State University. He has authored two books, *Comparison of the Training and Utilization of Scientists and Engineers in the U.S. and the U.S.S.R.*, with Catherine Ailes, for the National Science Foundation; and *Economics*, a forthcoming book (Dryden Press). In addition, he has published articles on economic education in the *Southern Social Studies Quarterly*, *Atlanta Magazine*, *Georgia Social Sciences Journal*, and *Dimensions*.

S. STOWELL SYMMES is Director, School Services Division, for the Joint Council on Economic Education. A former high school social studies teacher, he has JCEE responsibilities that include coordinating the Developmental Economic Education Program and the Master Curriculum Guide Project. He has conducted workshops for social studies teachers at local, state, and national levels. His publications include *Applying Economic Concepts: A Workbook for Students,* the *DEEP Handbook for Curriculum Change,* and articles in the *Indiana Social Studies Quarterly,* the *Business Education Forum,* and *Social Education.*

MARIANNE W. TALAFUSE is Associate Professor of Economics and Associate Director of the Center for Economic Education at Ball State University, Muncie, Indiana. She has had extensive workshop experience with both teachers and lay community leaders. Her publications include articles in *The Journal of Economic Education* and the *Journal of Cultural Economics.* She has earned awards for excellence in teaching economics and acclaim for her Indianapolis Children's Museum Project on Economics.

WILLIAM WALSTAD is Assistant Professor of Economics and Director of the Center for Economic Education at the University of Missouri, St. Louis. He has contributed articles to *Social Education, The Social Studies,* and *The Journal of Economic Education;* and he is a past recipient of awards from the International Paper Company Foundation Program for the Teaching of Economics. He was a high school social studies teacher and served as a research associate in economics while studying at the University of Minnesota. He is currently serving on the Research Advisory Committee of the National Council for the Social Studies and is a vice-president of the Missouri Council for the Social Studies.

DENNIS WEIDENAAR is Professor of Economics and Director of the Purdue Center for Economic Education. An active economic educator, he is interested in the expansion of basic economics instruction to social, professional, vocational, and educational groups throughout the country. In addition, he has focused on the improvement of teaching methodology. His recent research has been on the impact of economic education on employee attitudes and understanding of economic factors, and he has pioneered in the utilization and evaluation of tutorial video instruction in economics for college students. His publications include numerous articles in journals on economic education, textbooks, and monographs. He is on the editoral board of *The Journal of Economic Education.*

ELMER WILLIAMS is Associate Professor of Social Science Education and Associate Director of the Center for Economic Education at the University of Georgia. He has served on the Teacher Education Committee and Publications Board of the National Council for the Social Studies, and has contributed articles and chapters to several professional social science publications. As Associate Director of the Center for Economic Education, he conducts teacher education institutes and seminars and directs the Center's curriculum publications program. He has contributed to the development of several teacher resource manuals related to the *Trade-offs* television series.

In today's world, the arguments in favor of economic literacy are self-evident. It is impossible to pick up a newspaper, listen to the evening news, or try to make an intelligent decision at the polls without facing the need to understand economic terms and issues. This is the world for which schools are preparing young people. And while the science of economics is in itself "value-free," economic analysis, economic policy, and the economy itself are constantly intertwined with choices and decisions which reflect and are based on values. There is an integral relationship between a person's values and his/her economic choices. Economic literacy can assist people in improving their human capabilities, in making consumer choices, and in actively participating in private and public debate on crucial economic and political issues. There is also an integral relationship between issues of social justice and economics. Unless students understand the economic and social world in which they live, they will be unable to influence or change that world.

Sister Marie Herbert Seiter, C.S.J.
DEEP Coordinator,
Center for Economic Education,
College of St. Thomas, St. Paul, Minnesota

Courtesy of Arkansas State Council on Economic Education

A Framework for Cooperative Action

S. STOWELL SYMMES

Social studies educators and economic educators have a mutual interest in working together to achieve their educational objectives. Indeed, there is a commonality of goals so evident that to reject mutuality can only lead to unmet goals for both groups. The following two statements make this clear:

A BASIC RATIONALE FOR SOCIAL STUDIES EDUCATION

The basic goal of social studies education is to prepare young people to be humane, rational, participating citizens in a world that is becoming increasingly interdependent. The enhancement of human dignity through learning and commitment to rational processes as principal means of attaining that end are concerns shared with other disciplines. The other institutions of society also share with the schools a powerful influence upon the civic education of the young. Social studies education provides the only structured school or community focus for the preparation of citizens. A commitment to foster human dignity and rational process are keys to the structure of the social studies curriculum.

Human dignity means equal access to the rights and responsibilities associated with membership in a culture. In American culture, human dignity has long been sought through the struggle to implement ideas such as due process of law, social and economic justice, democratic decision making, free speech, religious freedom, self respect, and group identity. The idea of human dignity is dynamic and complex, and its definition likely to vary according to time and place. The essential meaning, however, remains unchanged: each person should have the opportunity to know, to choose, and to act.

Rational processes refer to any systematic intellectual efforts to generate, validate, or apply knowledge. They subsume both the logical and empirical modes of knowing as well as strategies for evaluating and decision making. Rationality denotes a critical and questioning approach to knowledge but also implies a need for discovering, proposing, and creating; the rational person doubts but also believes. The ultimate power of rational processes resides in the explicit recognition of the opportunity to decide for oneself in accord with the evidence available, the values one chooses, and the rules of logic. Therein lies the link between human dignity and the rational processes.

But without action, neither knowledge nor rational processes are of much consequence. This century has witnessed countless blatant violations of human dignity in the presence of supposedly well-educated populaces. It has been frequently asserted that knowledge is power; however, there is little evidence to assert that people who know what is true will do what is considered right. Commitment to human dignity must put the power of knowledge to use in the service of humanity. Whatever students of the social studies learn should impel them to apply their knowledge, abilities, and commitments toward the improvement of the human condition.

As knowledge without action is impotent, so action without knowledge is reprehensible. Those who seek to resolve social issues without concomitant understanding often tend not only to behave irresponsibly and erratically but in ways that damage their own future and the human condition. Therefore, knowledge, reason, commitment to human dignity, and action are to be regarded as complementary and inseparable.

NCSS *Social Studies Curriculum Guidelines*
Revised 1979

WHAT ARE THE OBJECTIVES OF ECONOMIC EDUCATION?

We take the objectives of economic education to be responsible citizenship and effective decision-making. But such a broad statement is only a beginning. What do we mean by responsible citizenship and effective decision-making? What kinds of economic issues and questions will high school graduates be most likely to confront as adults? How will their exposure to these issues and questions come about? And how will this shape the kinds of knowledge and skills they require to address these issues and questions?

High school graduates, as well as college graduates, will be exposed continuously over their lifetimes to a wide variety of economic questions. This will occur through their reading of newspapers and newsmagazines, their exposure to radio and television, their involvement in political campaigns and civic issues, and their participation in economic life as employees, employers, consumers, union members, and the like. The conclusions they reach on these issues will be reflected in how they vote; in the actions they take as members of unions, civic organizations and businesses; in their responses to appeals by the President and other public officials; and in economic decisions they make as individual consumers, workers, producers, savers, and investors. This means that the quality of individual decision-making is crucial to the effective operation of our social system and to the well-being of the individual.

Our purpose is to help to develop in young people, by the time they graduate from high school, an ability to understand and make reasoned judgments about major economic questions facing society and themselves as members of that society. Only in this way can they be responsible citizens and effective decision-makers.

JCEE *Master Curriculum Guide in Economics*
for the Nation's Schools, Part I, A Framework for
Teaching Economics: Basic Concepts 1977

It is relatively easy to recognize mutual interest. It is far more difficult to carry out the requisite tasks which assure goal achievement. This Bulletin was prepared to shed light on the complex curriculum process implied by the two statements quoted above. We speak to social studies educators, not as historians, political scientists, geographers, sociologists, anthropologists, or economists, but rather as teachers concerned with how these disciplines can help students to become flexible, humane, and autonomous individuals who can cope with the pressures of living in today's world.

There are some assumptions built into this Bulletin which should be made explicit at the outset. We accept the following:

• Formal schooling can make a difference in the capacity of students to cope with life, and the social studies curriculum is a powerful context for developing the requisite decision-making skills.

• Social studies educators are faced with limited time in which to make an impact on students in formal classroom settings, a fact making it necessary for them to select a few powerful instructional goals from among many valuable goals.

• Preparing students for more effective decision-making is one high-priority social studies goal that can be effectively achieved through economic education because of the unique characteristics of the economics discipline.

• Acquiring the skills of economic reasoning is a developmental task not accomplished by crash programs or single course "inoculations." This implies K–12 program development and, perhaps, lifelong learning expectations.

• In a democratic society, where virtually all citizens are free to choose alternative uses of limited resources, acquiring the skills of economic reasoning becomes an objective for *all students* of social studies.

• Curriculum development for more effective decision-making requires that social studies educators prepare clear, attainable, instructional objectives; transpose the objectives into effective classroom materials through adaptation and adoption; equip teachers with sufficient economics knowledge and instructional techniques to enable them to use instructional materials effectively; and be accountable for the curriculum decisions made by evaluating progress toward achieving objectives.

• Curriculum development is a constant "living" process and there are no "quick-fix" panaceas for achieving an ideal program.

We hope that this Bulletin will serve as a framework for marrying economic education to broad social studies objectives and that it will encourage specialists in other social science disciplines to forge similar ties. We have focused on links between economic education and the social studies because we believe economics is an important social science in the instructional mix. However, each social science discipline must contribute its unique share, but not to the exclusion of the others.

A distinguished member [Joan Robinson] of the Cambridge University economics faculty once said:

"The purpose of studying economics is not to acquire a set of ready-made answers to economic questions, but to learn how to avoid being deceived by economists."

I have some good friends who are economists and I am sure they could not object to Professor Joan Robinson's reference to ready-made answers . . . because there are no such answers. As for her warning about professional plausibility, I don't think her colleagues could object to this either—if, in some degree, it helps to broaden public understanding of basic economics— understanding based on an awareness of the economic facts of life, that would replace current misconceptions stemming from the interaction of fiction, emotion, and myth.

Frederick G. Jaicks
Chairman, Inland Steel Company
Chicago, Illinois

Courtesy of University of West Florida Information Services

CHAPTER 1

Economic Literacy— What Is It?

S. STOWELL SYMMES AND JUNE V. GILLIARD

Definitions of economic literacy abound. Among career educators and consumer educators the phrase may conjure up images of persons who know how to get jobs, how to run businesses, how to manage household incomes, how to balance budgets, how to invest savings, how to avoid signing "bad" consumer contracts, how to read and interpret stock market reports, and many other processes related to earning a living and allocating personal income. Such images may "turn off" social studies educators who consider economic literacy in terms of knowing how to interpret the economic causes of significant historical events, how to vote wisely on tax expenditures, how to evaluate government efforts to reduce inflation, how to explain the process of collective bargaining, how to compare the economic systems of two widely divergent nation-states, and much other knowledge about social issues.

These images suggest common characteristics that bridge apparent differences among various definitions of what it means to be literate in economics. Economic literacy is perhaps best defined in terms of a capacity to apply reasoning processes when making decisions about using scarce resources. Economic reasoning implies having the capacity to: define the choice-related problems which confront us; identify and rank criteria or goals which shape our choices; identify possible alternative choices; use knowledge (facts and concepts) to analyze the probable consequences of choosing each alternate; and take action based upon evaluation of the costs and benefits of various alternate choices.

Divergent views held by various constituencies such as business persons, labor leaders, economic educators, consumer activists, parents, back-to-basics advocates, career educators, and legislators account for much of the conflicting pressures placed on the schools in general and on social studies educators in particular. Pressures to "teach this" or "teach that" in the name of economic literacy are reflected in professional journal articles, school board directives, within-school departmental curriculum objectives, and legislative mandates shaped by pressure groups.

Obviously, no single definition will be acceptable to everyone who is concerned with economic education. Several years ago, Horton and Weidenaar used a Delphi-like procedure to explore the degree of consensus on a definition of the goals of economic education among more than 200 individuals representing both economics and social studies educators. Even among these relatively compatible groups, they found a wide disparity of emphasis. They produced a consensus statement as follows:

The aim of economic education is to improve our understanding of the worlds in which we live. Without this understanding we are frequently confused and unable to identify, analyze and interpret successfully the economic aspects inherent in so much about us. The goal reflects our conviction that comprehension of the economic realities of one's world enhances self-confidence and self-esteem. Accordingly, both intellectual and emotional barriers are lowered for the making of rational individual decisions, in the light of one's values, in both personal and social matters. Economics also provides frameworks and tools for rational individual discrimination among social alternatives, in the light of one's values. [It is hoped that] "better" social decisions will result.

(*The Journal of Economic Education,* Fall, 1975, p. 42)

Others who have written on the subject are quoted on the pages separating the chapters in this Bulletin. Each quote shows a particular facet of the elusive definition of economic literacy. Readers will want to digest and discuss these statements as they arrive at their own definitions. The process of having a social studies department agree upon a definition of economic literacy not only builds commitment to curriculum objectives, but also shapes the content and teaching strategies used to achieve those objectives.

The goals of economic education are highly compatible with the goals of social studies education. We are convinced that economic education can contribute significantly to the achievement of the goals outlined in the revised NCSS Social Studies Curriculum Guidelines. In fact, to the extent that social studies educators are committed to preparing students to become "humane, rational, participating citizens in a world that is becoming increasingly interdependent" (*Social Education,* April 1979, p. 262), they cannot avoid teaching economics.

In the 1980s and beyond, our nation will face a host of economic problems related to unemployment, inflation, energy, environmental pollution, and the role of government in the economic system. These problems are inextricably tied to the much broader issues of economic security, freedom, equity, and so forth. Many of the economic problems that must be dealt with are global in scope and are tied to such world-wide concerns as resource depletion, inadequate food supply, inequities in resource distribution, declining quality of life, and even survival of the human species. Attainment of the goal of humane, rational social participation will require that social studies programs provide opportunities for students to acquire proficiency in applying a body of tools that will allow them to deal with the economic aspects of complex social issues in a systematic and orderly way.

It is this body of tools that is economic education's unique contribution to the social studies program. It includes a set of basic concepts that allows one to recognize and articulate the economic dimensions of social problems and provides structure for the examination of specific economic issues. It also includes a set of procedures which improves one's ability to make reasoned, informed decisions about economic matters and to evaluate both personal and public actions.

Certainly, many of the issues confronting past, present, and future societies have non-economic dimensions that are as important as—if not more important than—their economic aspects. The integration of economic education in the social studies program, however, provides additional opportunities for broadening students' understanding of the human condition and for developing the abilities needed to cope with "real world" problems and issues.

If one cannot avoid economics in teaching social studies, the question facing school systems is not whether economic education should be included in the social studies curriculum. Rather, it is a question of the quality of economic education provided.

The quality of economic education in social studies programs is measured by the extent to which it contributes both to attaining specific social studies goals of knowledge, ability, valuing, and social participation, and to attaining the goal of economic literacy. Quality is in large part dependent upon the clarity of curriculum goals, teachers' knowledge and understanding of the potentials of economic education for broadening students' understanding of the real world, and the extent to which the experiences provided are attentive to student diversity, including differences in cultural backgrounds, interests, abilities, and learning styles.

The remaining chapters in this Bulletin focus on these and other problems related to the quality of economic education programs. They include suggestions for dealing with problems of goal definition, program development and implementation, and for evaluating progress toward stated curriculum goals. The authors describe various approaches to economic education and provide examples of classroom strategies that elementary and secondary teachers have found successful in helping students achieve specific program objectives.

Social studies teacher educators will also find ample material supporting the mutuality of their objectives and those of economic educators. A concluding chapter provides a perspective which argues that although substantial movement toward effective economic education programs has been made, much work remains. In fact, dealing constructively with the persistent problems of economic education is requisite for any effective social studies curriculum development process.

One of the goals of economic education is to provide the idea-base with which we think about economic and/or related issues; this is often referred to as the building of concepts. The learning of basic economic concepts or ideas forms a substantial part of the study of economics and is prerequisite to the successful acquisition of economic principles and problem-solving skills. Conceptualizing is a "freeing" type of learning, for it allows the learner to generalize the concept to new and different examples which were not included in instruction. . . . Concept attainment, then, provides a substantive framework which enables the learner to classify newly-encountered instances of the concept. In addition, concept attainment facilitates the ability to discern relationships between and among concepts, and aids the learner in identifying cause-effect relationships. Each of these skills plays a critical role in the attainment of a major goal of economic education, that of effective decision-making.

Beverly Jeanne Armento
Assistant Professor of Education
Georgia State University

Courtesy of the Arkansas State Council on Economic Education

CHAPTER 2

Developing Decision-Making Ability Through the Use of Economic Content

H. MICHAEL HARTOONIAN

Among the disciplines that are utilized in social studies education, economics is perhaps the most analytical. Its reliance upon mathematical models and attention to logic make it an appropriate area in which to develop and practice decision-making skills. In a very broad sense, and as the term is used here, decision-making may be thought of as trying to reach a conclusion about some event, action, object, idea or—more often—a series of these, which appear important enough to warrant our attention. More often than not, the use of decision-making skills or those mental operations we call "reasoning," which necessarily lead to some sort of conclusion, takes place unconsciously. My purpose here, however, is to make more explicit the skills and procedures involved in decision-making and to explore some classroom examples of successful lessons and strategies within the area of economics.

DECISION-MAKING AND REASONING

In its simplest form, the process of decision-making is related to stages of problem solving, which involve asking the questions:

1. What is the problem?
2. What are the alternatives?
3. Which alternative (consequence) is best?

This process, however, must include careful attention to the use and development of skills so that students *are able* to answer these questions. In other words, both the *form* and *content* of decision-making must be addressed. Thus, the component parts of the model that one uses to establish a more adequate process for decision-making might be somewhat arbitrary, but every good model must be concerned with two notions. First, it must present a set of necessary skills. Second, it must *sequence* those skills in such a way as to relate premises with conclusions and to relate problems with alternatives and consequences.

Skills become the necessary conditions of any decision-making model, while sequence or order gives sufficiency to the form component of decision-making. Therefore, we need both a set of skills and a sense of order (sequence) relative to the use of said skills. For example, one model sequence of the three steps delineated above is: (1) identifying the problem, (2) looking at alternative solutions, and (3) deciding which solution is best. A second model might expand the three steps into six steps:

1. Identify the issue or problem. What are the important facts? What questions of choice are raised?
2. Identify personal or broad social goals that apply to the problem. How would you rank them? (This might be done at some time other than during the decision-making process.)
3. Identify alternatives or possible solutions to the problem.
4. Decide which (economic) tools or concepts you need to analyze the alternatives.
5. Use the (economic) tools to analyze the alternatives. What will be the (economic) effect of each alternative? Which alternatives will meet the goals desired?
6. Evaluate which alternatives will best meet the goals as you ranked them. How much has to be given up in reaching one goal in order to reach another goal? What is your decision?[1]

There are other valid sequences which could be presented to give form to the decision-making process. But the key point to be made here is that in addition to "models," or forms, we must also pay attention to the skills that are used within these decision-making sequences. The necessary skills include conceptualizing, processing, and reasoning skills.[2]

Risk management and probability analysis are also decision-making skills which cannot be overlooked. For example, in a decision about taxation that involves increasing social security taxes as an alternative, the risk of impact on employment must be analyzed. This is both a quantitative and qualitative analysis, because risk is subject to both factors. We might argue that the risk of firms reducing employment due to increased social security is so unlikely that the risk is therefore quite small. Before deciding, however, this low probability of unemployment to individuals must be contrasted with the magnitude of the unemployment if and when it happens.

Economic problem-solving involves deciding what data are pertinent to the problem, collecting as many data as are feasible or necessary, organizing and presenting them, interpreting them, and finally using them to make the decision which is most likely to be correct. Probability and statistics provide us with

---

[1]Steps adapted from *Master Curriculum Guide, Part I, A Framework for Teaching Economics: Basic Concepts* by Lee Hansen, et al. Joint Council on Economic Education, p. 6.

[2]*Conceptualizing Skills*	*Processing*	*Reasoning*
Observing	Inferring	Deductive
Classifying	Predicting	Inductive
Seriation	Measuring	Analogical
Spatial Relationship	Formulating Definitions	
	Formulating Questions and Hypotheses	
	Testing Hypotheses	
	Formulating Models	

For a more detailed description of these skills, write to the author at: Wisconsin Department of Public Instruction, 125 South Webster Street, P. O. Box 7841, Madison, Wisconsin 53707.

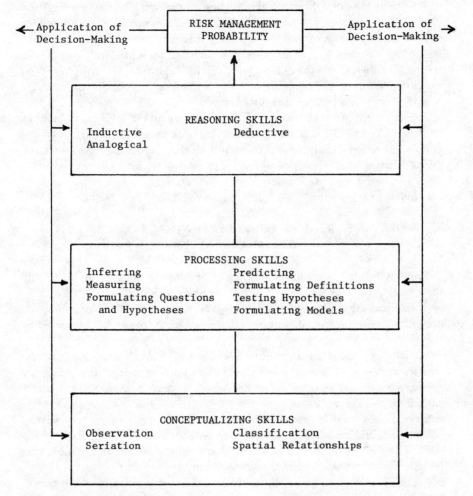

Figure 1 — **A Skill Network**

methods for solving problems in the face of uncertainties due to incomplete information.[3]

Once a set of thinking skills is delineated, it must then be organized if we expect to move *toward* reasoned decision-making in economic education. Figure 1 illustrates such a network of skills, showing that there is an interrelatedness and interdependence of the levels.

---

[3]Certain quantitative concepts are important for using probability in decision-making. They include descriptive statistics: percent, ratio, index number, mean, median, and mode; and inferential statistics: probability, chance, and sampling.

The levels of skills delineated here suggest a taxonomy for the development of reasoning abilities. The reasoning skills (inductive, analogical, and deductive) depend upon the various social studies processes (of inferring, predicting, measuring, formulating definitions, formulating questions and hypotheses, testing hypotheses, and formulating models) for substance. In turn, these processes depend upon the facilitating skills (of observation, classification, seriation, and spatial relationships) for existence.

These are the necessary and sufficient components of a decision-making model and its underlying skills. If students are to develop their decision-making abilities, teachers must give attention to both the "model" and its attendant "skills." Furthermore, practice with using the skills and the reasoning processes described here becomes necessary if we expect students to be competent decision-makers.[4]

THE NATURE AND USE OF ECONOMIC CONTENT IN DECISION-MAKING

Economics is a "natural" discipline for developing decision-making skills since its core concept is that of choice. Economic decisions deal with how limited resources are allocated among competing wants. There are many ways to organize the substantive content of economics. One framework is presented in Figure 2.[5]

Looking at the content in another way, we might say that economics deals with the *conversion* of inputs into outputs, the changing of production *possibilities* into goods and services, or the adding of "utility" to less useful items and situations (see Figure 3).

Since the production "possibilities" are always a function of our "conversion institutions," the possibilities vary among individuals and from society to society. The conversion institutions which "grease" the system and make it run include the subsystems of education, communications, transportation, banking, energy, and government. In this framework, economics is a way of thinking about the conversion of resources into more useful goods and services.

These schematics imply that students, by the time they graduate from high school, need to possess knowledge of a few analytical concepts drawn from the economics discipline, a few main economic institutions, and some key economic relationships. Without these conceptual tools, students will find it difficult to make thoughtful, reasoned choices about economic matters.

Learning to use these conceptual tools can begin in the primary school years, as is demonstrated by the sample classroom strategies which are included in this chapter. In fact, helping students to think through economic problems and make reasoned decisions is a task for teachers at all grade levels.

---

[4]H. Michael Hartoonian, "Reasoning as a Metaphor for Skill Development in the Social Studies Curriculum," *Theory and Research in Social Education,* Volume 7.

[5]From: *Master Curriculum Guide in Economics for the Nation's Schools, Part I, A Framework for Teaching Economic Basic Concepts,* (New York: Joint Council on Economic Education, 1977).

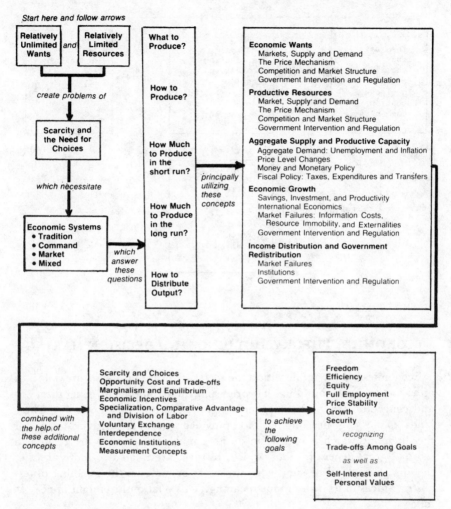

Figure 2 — **A Schematic Framework of Economics: An Approach to Linking the Concepts**

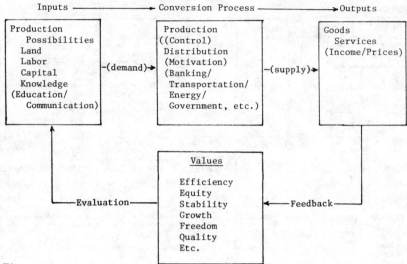

Figure 3

ECONOMICS, THEORY BUILDING, AND DECISION-MAKING

Economics is a discipline within the social sciences that pays a great deal of attention to theory building. Theories and their component generalizations and concepts form potentially meaningful structures of knowledge. These kinds of knowledge in economics have provided some of the analytical power of the discipline which is needed in decision-making. Concepts are related to more abstract generalizations, which, in turn, are related to more abstract theories. Each kind of knowledge subsumes or includes the meaning of less abstract ideas in its own unique meaning. This relationship might appear as follows:

THEORY

CIRCULAR FLOW OF INCOME

⇕

GENERALIZATIONS

What people spend on consumption and investment depends primarily on the income they receive.

Changes in the level of total spending (private consumption and investment along with government spending) will result in changes in employment and real output.

(continued on page 15)

Changes in the level of total spending will result in changes in the price level.

CONCEPTS

Price	GNP	Inflation	Saving
Money	Employment	Investment	
Production	Real output	Spending	

Such an organization of knowledge is meaningful because the components of knowledge interrelate and the structure relates to real-world phenomena and situations.

While concepts are the building blocks for thinking about the way in which the world is carved up into categories, generalizations are most useful here because they are the building blocks of decision-making. Some characteristics of generalizations include:

- All generalizations are statements asserting a claim.
- The claim identifies a relationship between examples of a concept and some specified factor.
- Sometime these statements of relationship are asserted in conditional form (if . . . then).
- All these statements of relationship imply or directly state a quantification claim.
- Quantifiers are either uniform or statistical (e.g., "all," "usually").
- The nature of the claim asserted can be reversible or irreversible, necessary or substitutable, or sufficient or contingent.

It is particularly the conditional statements (if . . . then) that provide the structure for establishing alternatives and their subsequent testing within the decision-making models. Conditional claims are the "work horses" of both deductive and inductive logic, and within economics there are numerous opportunities to formulate conditional statements worthy of testing.

It should be clear from the above that the vocabulary and logic of economics presents and represents decision-making. Decision-making in economics (questions/issues) can have both a personal as well as a system-wide character. Personal questions about purchasing item X or Y will have implications for aggregate demand, which, in turn, will help answer some of the system-wide questions of what and how much to produce. It should also be clear that the skills and decision-making models discussed above can be used with students in developing economic understandings, in analyzing economic issues of a personal or system-wide nature, and in developing better decision-making abilities. The following activities and those referenced by Talafuse and Weidenaar (Chapter 4) and Williams (Chapter 6) show how decision-making and economics flow together to form significant learning experiences for social studies students.

DECISION-MAKING STRATEGIES FOR CLASSROOM USE

Strategy No. 1 (Secondary)—A Team Approach to Economic Decision-Making.[6]

This strategy is part of a statewide economic contest sponsored by the Wisconsin Council for the Social Studies and the Wisconsin State Council on Economic Education. A school enters a team (or teams) of students to study and write out its analysis and policy statement. These statements are then judged by a panel of experts. The strategy is applicable within one school or class, with teams being selected within or between classes.

Rules.   This assignment provides two cases for you to analyze. For each case your task is to identify the issue or problem presented, identify alternative solutions to the problem, and use economic analysis to determine the best solution. For each case you must show *How* and *Why* you arrive at the decision you make.

A reasoned approach should be used. Before you begin to write answers to specific questions, you should organize your thinking and discussion by following these steps (another model can also be used).

1. Identify the issue or problem. What are the important facts? What questions of choice are related?
2. Identify personal or broad social goals that apply to the problem. How would you rank them?
3. Identify alternatives or possible solutions to the problem.
4. Decide which economic tools or concepts you need to analyze the alternatives.
5. Use the economic tools to analyze the alternatives. What will be the economic effect of each alternative? Which alternatives will meet the goals desired?
6. Evaluate which alternatives will best meet the goals as you ranked them. How much has to be given up in reaching one goal in order to reach another goal? What is your decision?

Each case requires you to answer one question, but your answer for each case should show how you followed through the steps to rational decision-making. The judges will not be looking for one right answer. They will look for how you arrive at your answer and how well you support it.

The cases will each count 50% in judging. There is no expected length for each answer. Allocate your time (one hour per case) and analyze each case as thoroughly as possible with this in mind. *Remember,* for each case you must show *How* and *Why* you arrive at your answer. An answer without these elements will count for very little.

GOOD LUCK!

---

[6]Lenore Burckel, *Examination: the 1980 Economics Contest,* for the WCSS.

Case One

PARKING LOT RATE CONTROL SOUGHT[7]

A Metro* councilman said yesterday he will ask the Metro Legal Department to draft an ordinance which would regulate "fluctuating" parking rates in private lots near the central business district.

"I don't know exactly what will be in the ordinance," said Councilman Frank Griffin. "I will just ask them to draw it up and to handle the legal aspects. I'm not even sure whether it can be done legally."

Griffin said he had given the parking problem much thought since the Metro Traffic and Parking Commission announced parking meter rate hikes Monday.

"If the downtown employees are going to be forced to park in private lots, they should be able to pay a fair rate," he said. "I often hear complaints from employees who say they can park in a lot for one rate during the first days of the week, but have to pay more on Friday because the lots have hiked their prices.†

"These parking people don't have set rates," he added. "One day they might charge 75 cents and the next day it might be $3."

Griffin, who said the legislation, if passed, would probably be enforced by the Traffic and Parking Commission, cited lots in the lower business district as examples of companies with fluctuating rates.

"They shouldn't change the prices simply because there's going to be 25,000 people in Nashville on a given weekend," he said.

Mary Carell, president of Central Parking System, which operates about 25 parking lots and garages in the central business district, said she didn't see how such legislation could be equitable.

"Parking prices are based on demand and location of parking facilities," she said. "People in the downtown area can drive two or three blocks from the core and find cheaper parking, but it won't be as convenient."

She said she believed the public should be informed in advance of parking rate hikes and that all lots should have their price lists posted in clear view.

"We welcome anyone's advice or thoughts on parking problems," she said.

The president of another major parking firm said he was not concerned with the legislation.

"My prices are the lowest in town except on weekends," said G. David Speights, president of Music City Parking. "We have price changes on weekends because we offer a different class of parking."

Music City operates several parking facilities near the Grand Ole Opry.‡

Speights denied that employees in the business district had to pay higher rates on Fridays and Saturdays.

"That legislation does not interest me one way or the other," Speights said. "I'm getting out of the parking business at the end of this year anyway."

---

*"Metro" refers to the Metropolitan Government of Nashville and Davidson County. The Metro Council is the legislative body.

†The number of people going to downtown Nashville (to shop or to work) is greater on Friday than on any other day of the week.

‡For the benefit of those who are not country music fans, Grand Ole Opry is a show put on every Friday and Saturday night in downtown Nashville that always plays to a full house, attracts numerous out-of-town visitors, and is known throughout the world. Inevitably, the demand for parking near Grand Ole Opry is greater on these nights than at any other time during the week.

Question: If the Metro Council has the legal power to regulate parking rates in any way it chooses, what do you think the Council's policy should be?

Hints to help you analyze the case:

Why do owners change their rates in the first place?

What are the economic effects of fluctuating prices? Who benefits? Who loses?

What options could be used to regulate the prices? What are the consequences?

In short, follow the steps of a decision-making model.

Case Two

Cries of anguish greeted the news on March 21, 1973, that the consumer price index in February had suffered the greatest one-month rise in twenty-two years. The rise of 0.8 percent (seasonally adjusted) was equivalent to an annual rate of increase of 9.6 percent. The biggest increase was registered by the food component, which jumped 2.4 percent — an annual rate of 28.8 percent. Senator William Proxmire, who had been urging a six-month freeze on all wages and prices, called the increase "shocking." George Meany, President of the American Federation of Labor and Congress of Industrial Organizations, urged Congress to impose mandatory price controls on food prices "from farm to market." This view was supported in the following editorial and attacked in the letter to the editor that comes after it.

JUMPY FOOD[8]

A funny thing about the healthy family appetite: it is somehow never appeased by a steady diet of soothing syrup in place of solid nourishment. It is all very pleasant to be told over and over by Administration experts that, if everybody just waits long enough, food prices will be coming down. But that doesn't fill any refrigerators or any stomachs either. Nor does it make it any easier to stretch the worker's paycheck at the supermarket checkout counter, even in this period of free-floating money.

The steep new climb registered by food prices last month, with meat, fish and poultry again the fastest climbers, is bound to make vastly more difficult the holding of the wage line in rubber, electrical manufacture, trucking, the postal service and all the other activities involved in the heavy 1973 round of collective bargaining. The settlements registered thus far have reflected a considerable effort on the part of organized labor to hold back a resumption of the wage-price leap-frog that leaves everyone a loser. But even these settlements are placed in jeopardy by the mad uprush of prices in the most basic part of every wage earner's budget.

It is past time for President Nixon to exhibit the same readiness to dump cherished shibboleths about what will or won't work in the economy that he showed when he unveiled his new economic policy more than a year and a half ago. Mandatory controls on food, starting at the farm level, will have the same profound and constructive effect that the initial freeze did in restoring confidence among workers and all other consumers and in helping to sustain the buying power of the domestic dollar.

---

[8]The editorial appeared in *The New York Times*, March 11, 1973, page 42. The letter is from the same newspaper, April 5, 1973. Copyright © 1973 by the New York Times Company. Reproduced by permission.

TO THE EDITOR:

We agree with your March 22 editorial, "Jumpy Food," that it is time for President Nixon "to dump cherished shibboleths about what will or won't work" and adopt "mandatory controls on food starting at the farm level"—but not for the reasons you give. The modern generation lacks experience with the price controls of World War II. As educators, we want it to learn by experience that price controls on farm products will necessitate rationing of foods by the Government, that rationing will lead to black markets, that black markets will undermine price control and that the cure will be worse than the disease.

RENDIGS FELS
T. ALDRICH FINEGAN
Nashville, March 23, 1973

Question: Should the President adopt mandatory price controls on food prices at all levels "from farm to market"?

Hints to help you analyze the case:

What policy option to fight inflation is suggested here?

What are the consequences of not using this policy?

What are the consequences of using this policy?

Are there other policy options available?

What are the consequences of the various policy options?

In short, follow the steps of a decision-making model.

Strategy No. 2 (Secondary)—Allocating Energy Resources—The Market System v. Command.[9]

In a recent Gallup Poll, over half of the American people surveyed wanted gasoline rationing by coupons rather than by higher prices. Will coupon rationing work, or will higher prices discourage inefficient use and encourage increased production of energy? The following Cases (Strategies) can be used in units on supply and demand theory.

Case One—What If?   In order to examine the effects of higher energy prices on different sectors of the economy, have your students step into the shoes of various economic decision-makers. Have them react to higher energy prices. Here are some examples that relate to just one form of energy—natural gas.

Role 1—You are the president of a natural gas company. The government says that you can charge only a certain amount for natural gas. This amount barely covers your costs. What decisions would you make concerning exploration for new sources of natural gas? Now the government says you can sell your natural gas for whatever customers will pay for it. What decisions would you make concerning exploration for new sources of natural gas? What effects, if any, would the amount of competition in the natural gas industry have on your decision?

Role 2—You are the president of a company that uses large quantities of natu-

---

[9]Economic Topic Series: John S. Morton, *The Economics of the Energy Problem* (New York: Joint Council on Economic Education).

ral gas. What types of decisions will you face when natural gas prices go up? Will you raise the prices of your products? What factors would you consider in deciding whether to raise the prices of your products? Will you change your production techniques?

Role 3—You own a home that is heated with natural gas. What decisions do you face when natural gas prices go up? What changes, if any, would you make in your life style? What changes, if any, would you make in your home?

Case Two—Demand Elasticities.   After a lesson on elasticity of demand, students can investigate the elasticity of demand for energy forms. Have higher prices for gasoline, electricity, and natural gas cut the sales of these products? What is the historic growth rate for consumption of these products? What has happened to the growth rate since price increases? Since sales have slackened, is this because of higher prices, the recession, or both?

Case Three—The Price Mechanism and Equity.   To illustrate the effect of energy price increases on various income groups, pass out this chart compiled from statistics taken from the Ford Foundation Energy Project report.

Income Group	Percentage of Income Spent on Electricity, Natural Gas, and Gasoline (1972–73)
Poor (average income $2,500)	15
Lower middle (a.i. $8,000)	7
Upper middle (a.i. $14,000)	6
Well-off (a.i. $24,500)	4

Now ask questions such as the following:
1. Who is hurt most by energy price increases?
2. What are some of the ways the burden of energy price increases can be reduced for low income families?
3. For whom is there greater elasticity of demand for energy: low income groups or high income groups? Justify your answer.

Case Four—Pay a "Complement" to the Substitute.   Have students make a study of energy as a complementary good. Complementary goods are those which are used jointly—such as tires and automobiles or gasoline and automobiles. Note the graph (right), which shows the relationship between the rise in the price of fuel and the rise in the basic round-trip economy fare between New York and London on a major United States airline.

In what situation is energy a complementary good? What has been the significance of this for the American consumer? (For example, as gasoline prices soared in late 1973 and 1974, motor vehicle usage dropped sharply.) How would schools and colleges have been affected? Homeowners?

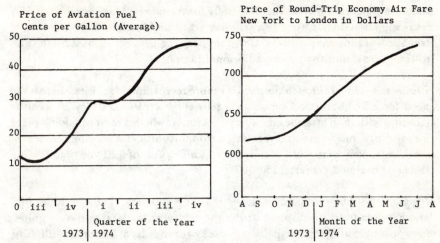

Direct students to do research on how the energy crisis affected substitute products. For example, as the price of oil rose, so did the price of coal, a substitute product. (In December 1973, coal was selling for less than $14 per ton to utilities; by May 1974, its price was about $26 per ton.)

Strategy No. 3 (Secondary)—City Council Simulation.[10]

You are a member of the City Council in a city of 100,000 people. Over the past ten years the city has had a population growth of about 20 percent. In order to provide the needed additional services, it has been necessary to increase the property tax rate for the past two years. Citizens are becoming angry about continuing increases.

The funds for the most urgent items in the budget for the forthcoming year have already been appropriated. There is approximately $1.5 million left to allocate and twelve important programs that various citizens groups have urged the council to approve:

Proposal 1 — One area of the city does not have adequate fire protection. A home in that area burned down in the past year, and a small child was badly hurt. Citizens in the area have written, phoned, and appeared at the budget hearings to request better fire protection. Cost for additional fire personnel: $200,000.

Proposal 2 — Problems with teenagers have been increasing. Vandalism is on the rise, parents are concerned about the mounting use of drugs, and the police are dealing with more runaways. The City Council would like to start a new juvenile division in the Police Department to help keep youngsters out of trouble. Cost for a social worker, two police officers, and a secretary: $100,000.

Proposal 3 — The city has inadequate recreational facilities, and much of what is available is in very bad condition. One group of citizens feels that more

[10]From *Master Curriculum Guide in Economics for the Nation's Schools, Part II, Strategies for Teaching Economics and Consumer Education* (Secondary) (New York: Joint Council on Economic Education, 1979).

should be spent on recreation, especially for teenagers. More opportunity for recreational activities, they say, will pay off in a reduction in the number of teenagers getting into trouble. Cost for repairing the tennis, basketball, and softball areas, and for paying additional personnel: $250,000.

Proposal 4 — In addition to the need for more recreational facilities, there is the need for a neighborhood center in a particular area of the city. A wealthy citizen is willing to give the city a large mansion, which would provide a place for meetings, programs, and recreational opportunities for everyone from pre-schoolers to senior citizens — if the city can staff it. Cost of staff and maintaining the neighborhood center: $350,000.

Proposal 5 — The city landfill site is reaching capacity. The city must find another area for trash disposal within the next year. Federal and state guide-lines no longer allow municipalities to use low or marshy areas for landfill. Cost of using an out-of-town landfill site: $200,000.

Proposal 6 — One section of the city has developed very rapidly, and sewer lines are at capacity. Citizens are complaining about the unpleasant odors, and many think that a satellite treatment plant is needed. Federal funds will pay for building the plant, but the community will have to pay for its operation. Cost of one year's operation of a treatment plant: $300,000.

Proposal 7 — Three streets in the city are unpaved and many contain large potholes. When it rains, the unpaved streets are muddy and all but impassable. In dry weather the dust is thick, and some citizens feel the dust to be a definite health hazard. Several citizens have broken automobile axles when hitting potholes. Cost of upgrading those streets: $500,000.

Proposal 8 — In one part of town the houses are rundown but could be rehabili-tated. Wiring, plumbing, general carpentry work, roofing, etc. would make the houses more livable and improve the neighborhood's appearance. Some citizens have recommended that local money be given to poor citizens so that they could rehabilitate their homes. Cost to fix up the most rundown houses: $300,000.

Proposal 9 — City employees are feeling the pinch of the rising cost of living. They are demanding a 10 percent raise. Estimated cost of employee pay raise for the first year: $200,000.

Proposal 10 — A lovely creek runs through the center of the city. Over the years it has been silting up, and as a result one residential section has a flooding problem. Homeowners there are demanding that the city dredge the creek to prevent flooding. Cost of dredging and fixing up the banks: $150,000.

Proposal 11—Citizens want educational standards to be upgraded. School officials say they can improve education in basic skills and career placement if they employ a specialist at each grade level. Cost of new personnel: $300,000.

Proposal 12—The city has a high rate of teenage unemployment. Citizens have said there is a need to develop activities and meaningful work experiences for this age group. Much interest and support for a summer employment program exists. Cost for the summer employment program: $150,000.

ESTIMATED TOTAL COST OF ALL PROGRAMS . . . $3,000,000

You have been a good Council member, one who tries to study the issues and is concerned about the welfare of all the members of your community. You would also like to be re-elected. Which combination of programs totalling approximately $1,500,000 do you think is the best alternative for the community? Use the Budget Analysis Worksheet as a guide while making your decision.

After individual decisions are made, the whole Council must decide on how the funds will be allocated.

BUDGET ANALYSIS WORKSHEET

Prepared by _____ Date _____

Name(s)

Step 1: Define the problem (Why does a choice have to be made?)

Step 2: Specify alternatives (What are some possible choices?)

Step 3: State the criteria (How will the alternatives be evaluated?)

Step 4: Evaluate the alternatives (How good is each alternative?)

Step 5: Make a decision (Which alternative is best and why?)

Strategy No. 4 (Elementary)—White Elephant Auction.[11]

Concepts: Decision-making, opportunity cost, allocation of limited resources, market-clearing prices

Materials: Auction items, envelopes, play money

Time: One hour

---

[11]This lesson appeared as part of an article published in May, 1980 by *The Elementary Economist*. It is a national newsletter published by the National Center of Economic Education for Children, Lesley College, Cambridge, Massachusetts.

Procedure—About two weeks before the auction, ask children to bring to school "white elephants" from home, items which are still in good condition, but which their families no longer find useful. Keep the items on display in the classroom as they are brought in. Announce to the class members that they will have an opportunity to "purchase" these items on a certain date with money which you will give to them, and that they will be allowed to take their purchases home to keep.

Prepare for each pupil a sealed envelope containing amounts of play money from $15 to $25 and distribute the envelopes randomly on the morning of the sale. Arrange for someone to act as a record-keeper for the sale to keep track of the items sold, the buyers, and the amounts paid for each item. The teacher may act as the auctioneer, setting the minimum bids and accepting whole dollar bids only.

At the end of the auction, discuss the experience with the class, using the following guidelines:

1. How did the supply (quantity) of various items affect your purchasing plans? How did it affect your purchasing power?
2. What were your personal *opportunity costs* during this auction? An *opportunity cost* is defined as the second best alternative you had to give up so that you could have your first choice(s).
3. What can you say about the desirability of items which were scarce? Of items which were plentiful? How did the conditions of supply affect the *market clearing price;* that is, the price at which the demand dropped off?
4. How did your *limited resources* (certain amount of money) affect your purchasing plans and your purchasing power?
5. As you looked over the items before the sale, you probably developed some sort of strategy for using your money. Write a one-page description of that strategy, along with an assessment of how well it worked. What things would you do differently if we had another auction? Why?

Strategy No. 5 (Elementary)—Showing Global Interdependence.

Concepts: Global interdependence, utility, allocation of resources

Materials: Large map of the world or paper of sufficient size to have students draw their own map of the world, magazines or drawing paper

Time: Three hours, over a three-day period

Procedures—Have students make a list (in pictures taken from magazines or drawn) of items or products (or parts of products) which come from other countries. Display these pictures in the room under the appropriate heading: PRODUCTS WE USE FROM OTHER LANDS.

Have students develop a map of the world (or published map) and attach a string from the item or product's geographic source to your local community; in other words, identify the country from which the item comes and mark that country on the map of the world. Then run a string from that mark to your local community.

Have the students develop a "world factory" to produce a product. Have them deal with questions of: (a) where to locate the factory or factories, (b) where to get the labor to work in the factory, and (c) how to distribute the product. Brainstorm other questions that need to be answered.

Strategy No. 6 (Elementary)—Production/Productivity

Concepts: Decision-making, production, productivity, assembly line, division of labor, specialization, efficiency, factors of production

Materials: Scrap paper, scissors, magic marker, paper clips, ruler

Time: One hour

Procedure — Establish from three to six "factories" in your classroom. Have a different number of students in each factory.

Factory A	Factory B	Factory C	Factory D
•	• •	• • •	• • • •

Product

Decide on producing the same product in each of the established factories. For example, a piece of paper with four stars drawn on it, folded in a special way and paper-clipped.

PRODUCTION PROCESS

For production, each factory will need: land (table), raw materials (paper), labor (students), capital (scissors, paper clips, magic marker, etc.), and management (strategy, organization) for production.

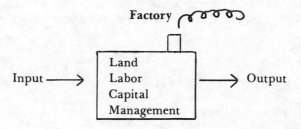

Factory

Input ———→ | Land · Labor · Capital · Management | ———→ Output

Have students decide on how they want to set up their individual factories and begin the production process. Establish a time (three minutes)— "rounds"—for the factories to work, and keep track of the output during each of these three-minute periods. You should post the results of each factory's output for each of the rounds.

Factory	Round 1	Round 2	Round 3	Round 4	Etc.
A					
B					
C					
D					

1. What is the production of factory A, B, C, D for each of the rounds?
2. What is the productivity (output divided by number of workers) for each factory? Tools are a constant.
3. How would you organize your factory to increase productivity?
4. How can you effectively take account of the quality control of a product?
5. Are there any risk factors involved in each factory?

CONCLUSION

The secondary and elementary lessons listed above involve students in decision-making activities through the context of economic issues. As students learn to make decisions, it is important for teachers to place continually before them decision-making models that provide opportunities to develop reasoning skills, to increase their understanding of probability and risk management, and to extend their knowledge of the vocabulary and logic of economics. These factors taken together will help students to become better decision-makers. Above all, students must *practice* decision-making under the watchful eyes of social studies teachers who understand both the form and content of decision-making.

In our concern for improving economic education, it's all too easy to lose sight of the goals of economic activity. These goals, as I see it, are human welfare, human happiness and human dignity.

And, I might add, these are the goals of the labor movement—the welfare, happiness, and dignity of working people and their families.

With these thoughts in mind, let me suggest two key goals of economic education. (1) Economic education should help young people and adults to make intelligent individual occupational decisions. (2) Economic education should help people to become good citizens, competent to make intelligent decisions in economic, social and political affairs.

I believe economic education must increase its emphasis on collective bargaining in labor-management relations because collective bargaining in labor-management relations gives us knowledge, skills and experience in conflict resolution that are transferable to other areas of our economic, social and political life—knowledge, skills and experience that are needed to resolve the economic, social and political conflicts that inevitably come along in a democratic society."

Markley Roberts
Economist, AFL-CIO

Building an Effective Economic Education Program Using Principles of Successful Adoption and Implementation

CAROLE L. HAHN AND FRANCIS W. RUSHING

One way to improve the economic literacy of citizens is to revise the school curriculum to include more economics. Revision can occur as a result of a comprehensive study of what ought to be taught and how, or it can be approached by making small incremental changes as opportunities arise. In this chapter, we will describe both total and incremental approaches to improve economic education and suggest strategies to readers who are contemplating curriculum changes.

In changing the economics dimension of the school curriculum through a total approach, one might consider the four questions posed by Ralph Tyler (1949) and adopted by many curriculum developers:

1. What educational purposes should the school seek to attain?
2. What educational experiences can be provided which are likely to attain these purposes?
3. How can these educational experiences be effectively organized?
4. How can we determine whether these purposes are being attained?

In order to answer the first question, curriculum specialists suggest that one consider four sources: the discipline, society's needs and values, the needs of the learners, and the learning process. Most curriculum writers also suggest that the second question be answered as a list of goals and objectives. The answer to the third question leads to the development of courses, units of study, and learning activities; and the response to the last question is a description of the evaluation procedures which provide feedback to the curriculum system. Figure 1 is typical of most models for curriculum development.

With attention to the various components of the curriculum development process, the Joint Council on Economic Education (JCEE) has designed an approach to curriculum change—the Developmental Economic Education Program, more commonly known as the D.E.E.P. Model.

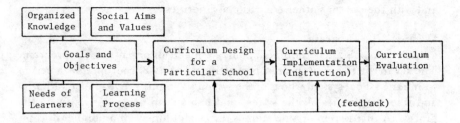

Figure 1—**Curriculum Development Model**[1]

D.E.E.P.—A TOTAL APPROACH

The D.E.E.P. model was developed by the Joint Council on Economic Education for the purpose of modifying the K-12 curriculum to include a larger amount of economics and to increase the quality of the instructional program in economics already in the curriculum.[2] The Joint Council began to develop the D.E.E.P. model in 1964 with an experiment involving 29 school systems, and since that time the model has been revised and used in hundreds of school systems across the United States.

D.E.E.P. curriculum change is predicated upon the concept that each stage in the curriculum development process is, in some way, related to the other stages. Thus, the change process is one which requires a systematic plan whereby each of the elements is considered in order to move toward the desired goals. D.E.E.P. was designed to be a flexible systematic approach which would permit school systems to tailor changes in their economic education curriculum to their unique situation. The six stages of the D.E.E.P. model are:

1. Determine goals in economic education.
2. Establish a plan to obtain these goals.
3. Organize the program.
4. Implement the program.
5. Evaluate the program.
6. Institutionalize the change into an ongoing program of the school system.

Determine the Goals

The goals for D.E.E.P. are determined by a committee of persons composed of school representatives, business persons, economic education specialists, labor leaders, and other involved community leaders. The goals are specified as outcomes which are to be achieved in a particular period of time. They must be

[1]J. Galen Saylor and W.M. Alexander, *Planning Curriculum for Schools* (New York: Holt, Rinehart and Winston, 1974), pp. 23-27.

[2]S. Stowell Symmes, ed., *Handbook for Curriculum Change* (New York: Joint Council on Economic Education, 1969).

realistic goals, compatible with the resources available to the school system, and with the system's other educational priorities.

Organize the Program

Once the goals are determined, plans are made for organizing the program. The key to the D.E.E.P. process is selecting a D.E.E.P. coordinator, a person within the school system who is in the system's administrative line of authority and who coordinates all the system and non-system persons involved in the process. A first step in organization is the establishment of a number of committees which provide guidance and ensure support for the curriculum change process. These committees, like the one which established the goals, are composed of a cross-section of the community.

An important role in the D.E.E.P. process is played by economic education specialists from local centers for economic education and by other special consultants in fields such as curriculum design, materials development, and testing and evaluation. These persons supplement the personnel within the system and assist in both the designing of the program and in the training of system personnel who will be responsible for the implementation of the program. Sometimes these outside specialists are not only necessary but critical in the early stages of the D.E.E.P. process. However, as the process develops, the system becomes less dependent on outside consultants.

Implement D.E.E.P.

At this stage the project conducts teacher-training, develops teaching materials, and writes new curriculum materials or modifies old ones. The nature and extent of the materials development and the types and grade-level of teacher-training will depend upon the curriculum design and on the local school needs. Generally, the implementation occurs over a three-year period, with components being introduced as the implementation plan specifies. The D.E.E.P. process has been introduced at grade one and then systematically extended to the higher grades. In other systems, it has been introduced at the secondary level, due to mandated courses, and then extended down to lower grades to build skills necessary to make the required instruction effective. The rationale for the implementation sequence will vary from system to system.

Evaluate the Program

Any educational program must result in positive progress toward its stated goals. D.E.E.P. builds in a feedback process for continuous evaluation of the stages of the program. Progress can be measured in terms of the numbers of teachers who receive economic education training, quantity and quality of materials developed or adapted for the curriculum, and student performance on evaluation instruments which measure achievement in mastering economic concepts and generalizations.[3] The evaluation components should relay signals as to the strengths and weaknesses of the curriculum design and implementation process and provide guidance on what and how adjustments to the design should be made.

---

[3]See Chapter 6 of this Bulletin for examples of evaluation techniques.

Institutionalize Economic Education

The ultimate goal of curriculum change is to transform what begins as a special project or a pilot program into an integrated part of the school system's curriculum. The institutionalization will occur only if the goals are generally accepted as desirable, if the curriculum design is effective in meeting the goals, and if there is tangible evidence that the student acquires knowledge and skills which can be utilized. Finally, there must be key persons within and outside the system who are willing to use these positive characteristics and outcomes of D.E.E.P. to defend it against the ever-increasing demands of other subjects or topics for time and space in the curriculum.

The implementation of the total D.E.E.P. process requires the acquiring and utilization of a variety of resources. These are obtained from the school system, the Joint Council on Economic Education and its affiliated councils and centers, and the local community organizations. Not only must financial and human resources be tapped to initiate D.E.E.P., but its final success, the institutionalization of economic education, requires sustained funding. This can be obtained only if measured progress toward achieving the goals of D.E.E.P. can be demonstrated. D.E.E.P. must always remain flexible so that it can adapt to the changing structure and needs of a school system.

There is little doubt that the D.E.E.P. model has resulted in increased economics instruction in school systems which have adopted it. Evidence to support this contention is the number of teachers trained, the proliferation of non-economic education instructional materials, the numbers and level of economics courses, and the school curriculum documents which show grade placement of instructors of economic concepts.[4]

Several research papers have been written which attempt to measure quantitatively the impact of D.E.E.P. on the learning of economics. One such study by William B. Walstad and John C. Soper found that "students in D.E.E.P. schools, on average, appear to have a higher score on the standardized Test of Economic Literacy; hold a more positive attitude toward economics as a subject; exhibit a greater degree of economic sophistication in comparison to non-D.E.E.P. students."[5] The authors state that the "reasons for these positive, significant effects may be due to the impact of teacher-training programs on D.E.E.P. schools or the stimulating curriculum program implemented in D.E.E.P. systems."[6] This study concludes that the D.E.E.P. process has a positive impact on *both* the cognitive and affective domains.

While the D.E.E.P. model has proven to be effective in many schools over the years, we recognize that changing curriculum or instruction to improve economic experiences does not always occur through such a total process involving a whole school system. Often incremental changes are made as new courses are mandated, new textbooks are adopted, or a teacher picks up an idea for a new lesson at a state social studies convention or from *Social Educa-*

[4]"Survey of Economic Concepts Taught in Rome/Floyd County Area Schools" (Preliminary Report). Berry College Center for Economic Education, Summer, 1980, mimeographed.

[5]William B. Walstad and John C. Soper, "A Model of Economics Learning in the High Schools." Paper presented at the Allied Social Science Association Meetings, Denver, Colorado, September, 1980.

[6]*Ibid.*, p. 16.

tion magazine. Whether one is introducing the idea that a school system under-take the total D.E.E.P. approach or purchase a new set of student materials, we believe that people are more likely to be successful in their change efforts if they consider several principles derived from research on educational change and from the experiences of others who previously instituted economic education programs. Teachers, department heads, supervisors, and professors who want to introduce new ideas, practices, or materials in economics education need not "reinvent the wheel." By making systematic plans and keeping a few principles in mind, one's efforts are more likely to result in successful changes than if one just rushes in without such planning. Figure 2 outlines the principles to be considered at each stage of the process.

Figure 2—**Principles To Consider at Each Stage of Change Process**

Awareness	Persuasion	Trial and Adoption	Implementation
Felt Need	Compatibility with needs and values	Training and Materials	Continuous Training Continuous Monitoring
	Reduce complexity	Principal's support	Mutual Adaptation Advocates
	Need support of Opinion Leaders, Gatekeepers, and potential Advocates.		

INTRODUCING CHANGE

Create a Felt Need

People do not make changes unless they feel a need to change.[7] To stimulate educators and community people to feel a need to improve economic education, it is often important to demonstrate that their students are not sufficiently economically literate. To document that generalization, one can obtain data from locally administered tests of economic understanding. Armed with such evidence, state councils and centers of economic education have launched low-key campaigns to "create a felt need" and to rally support for improving economics education in local schools.

To create awareness of a need, one might combine a local needs assessment with an audio-visual presentation or a brochure about the goals of economic education. Several state councils of economic education, such as North Carolina and Louisiana, developed a packet of materials to convince audiences of the need for D.E.E.P.[8]

When school boards mandate new economics courses or require competencies in economics for high school graduation, school faculties feel a need to revise their curriculum and to increase their knowledge of economics. While we

[7]Ronald Havelock, *Planning for Innovation Through Dissemination and Utilization of Knowledge* (Ann Arbor: University of Michigan, 1971).

[8]Louisiana Council on Economic Education, "Developmental Economic Education Program: A Guide for Implementation," 1979; and North Carolina Council on Economic Education and the North Carolina Department of Public Instruction, "The Developmental Economic Education Program in North Carolina," 1978.

are not advocating mandated changes, we recognize that such demands often create felt needs to improve economics; economic educators can capitalize on such needs. Teachers, curriculum coordinators, and college professors of economics and of education can assist with curriculum revision, and college courses and staff development programs can be offered to meet recognized needs.

The textbook-adoption cycle offers opportunities to improve economic education, but unless decision-makers feel a need to make changes, this opportunity will be missed. A recent national study reports that, for the most part, teachers are satisfied with their textbooks.[9] To stimulate consideration of new alternatives, one might ask decision-makers to compare textbooks, with attention to criteria like the following: Are major economic concepts adequately presented and reinforced? Is there evidence that students who use the material do better on tests of economic understanding than do students who use other materials?

After having read this Bulletin, one might feel a need to expose students to more extreme ideologies, or to give them practice in the decision-making approaches that H. Michael Hartoonian suggests. In order to make the changes, you may want to share the appropriate chapters with colleagues, so that they, too, will feel a need to change.

Efforts are needed to work for the improvement of economic education precisely because many people are satisfied with the status quo. To create a climate conducive to change, one must begin by convincing decision-makers that there is a need to modify the curriculum, instructional activities, materials, or teacher preparation.

Persuade with Attention to Needs, Values, and Complexity

After people have been made aware of a need for economic education or for a better alternative, they need to be persuaded to try something new through more personal forms of communication. At the persuasion stage in the change process, it is important to demonstrate that the proposed new approach is *compatible with the needs and values* of the people who are considering it.[10] If the principal values public relations with the community, then one must explain how the new program will be good "P.R." If teachers are concerned about student reading or mathematics achievement, then they must be shown how the economics program will produce gains in those areas. One teacher may value students' learning how to cope in the real world, while another values developing their critical thinking, and yet a third values their learning the facts of history. One must appeal to each person's particular concerns. Often teachers value student interest,[11] so it is particularly important to show that the new

[9]Douglas Superka, Sharryl Hawke, and Irving Morrissett, "The Current and Future Status of the Social Studies," *Social Education*, Volume 44, May, 1980, pp. 366-67.

[10]Everett M. Rogers with F. Floyd Shoemaker, *Communication of Innovations: A Cross-Cultural Approach* (New York: Free Press, 1971); and Carole L. Hahn, "Attributes and Adoption of New Social Studies Materials," *Theory and Research in Social Education*, March, 1977.

[11]Hahn, *ibid.*, and Gerald Marker, "Why Schools Abandon New Social Studies Materials," *Theory and Research in Social Education*, March, 1980.

approach will appeal to students.

The position of the centers for economic education has been that the existing curriculum ought to be enhanced to include more and better economics. This approach has been to show how learning economics concepts is compatible with developing skills in mathematics, reading, and writing, and with learning historical and political science concepts.[12]

When economic education is presented not as indoctrination but as the use of economic concepts and of a process for making decisions, it is compatible with many widely held values: democratic decision-making, objective analysis, the development of critical thinking, and the application of current scholarship to the lives of youth. On the other hand, if economic education prescribes particular policies, it will be incompatible with the values of those who hold opposite positions and with those who believe students ought to practice democratic decision-making.

In persuading people to make changes in economic education, it will be necessary, but not sufficient, to demonstrate that the changes will be compatible with their needs and values. They must be convinced also that the changes will not be difficult to understand, to use, or to do. Research on educational changes indicates that innovative ideas, practices, and materials are most likely to be adopted when they are perceived to be uncomplicated.[13]

Teachers who are not trained in economics or who feel uncomfortable with the subject are not likely to be willing proponents of the teaching of more economics. Their anxieties can be reduced with the promise of in-service training, "how-to" teachers' guides, and assistance from others as problems arise. Examples of overcoming perceived complexity can be seen in the experiences of many D.E.E.P. programs. Economic education centers and D.E.E.P. coordinators provide needed training. Also, they supply simple but effective "how to" and "with what" guides and procedures, and they offer consulting assistance to teachers undertaking the changes.

Often teachers are hesitant to try new materials or approaches because they are concerned about difficulties in management. That kind of perceived complexity can also be reduced by anticipating it in advance. If the economics program *Trade-Offs* comes on television at an inconvenient time, suggestions could be made for taping the program or making schedule adjustments. If teachers hesitate to use simulations to make economics principles concrete, one can explain how noise can be reduced and how materials can be easily made, and can offer to go through the step-by-step guide with the teachers so that they will see how it will run. It is important to put oneself in the other person's shoes and think of all the ways that he or she might see the change as being difficult and then plan suggestions to reduce such concerns.

To reduce the perceived complexity of using economic analysis and decision-making, one can suggest that teachers begin by using the lessons contained in

---

[12]Examples of publications are the Joint Council on Economic Education, *Learning Economics through Childrens' Stories,* and *Teaching Economics in American History;* and the University of Georgia Center for Economic Education, *Improving Comprehension and Vocabulary Development in Economics.*

[13]Brenda J. Turnbull, Lorraine I. Thorn, and C. L. Hutchins, *Promoting Change in Schools* (San Francisco: Far West Laboratory for Educational Research and Development, 1974).

Chapters 2, 4, and 5 before they start designing their own. And to reduce anxiety about using ideologies, teachers can participate in sessions on handling controversial issues which use the materials recommended by Jack Nelson and Kenneth Carlson.

In planning a strategy to create interest in improving economic education, one must consider the perspectives of many different people. It is helpful to use the "market segmentation" used in business.[14] Consider the different groups whose support is needed, and plan different approaches to match the particular needs, values, and concerns for complexity of each of those distinct groups. Special attention should be given to individuals whose support is crucial to the change process. Research on the diffusion of innovations in education suggests that there are three important roles to consider — Inside Advocates, Opinion Leaders, and Gatekeepers.

Roles to Consider

Inside Advocates are people within the system who will see it in their interest to have the school adopt the innovation. They are the ones who persist in championing the idea when it might otherwise die.[15] Supervisors or economic education center directors, who are not themselves part of the school faculty, will need to be sure that there is an advocate in the school to continue to promote the change. Individuals who have previously shown interest in or support for economic education have the potential to be useful Inside Advocates. Department heads or teachers who want to institute changes may themselves serve as Inside Advocates.

Economic educators have developed several methods of recruiting Inside Advocates. They work with business men and women on school boards or who are active in parent organizations. They frequently recruit teachers by offering low-cost courses which provide the credits teachers seek for graduate degrees, certification, or salary raises. Once enrolled in the course, the teachers are won over to the importance, challenge, and enjoyment of teaching economics. Educators who are thus convinced often become advocates in their school systems for improving economic education.

The primary role of the D.E.E.P. coordinator is to serve as an Inside Advocate for economics within a school system. With numerous demands on the school system, it is the D.E.E.P. coordinator who continues to speak for economics as a priority. Sometimes the coordinator is appointed by the superintendent as a result of the commitment of the central office. Often the person volunteers out of his or her own commitment and is given the title "coordinator" to sanction the role of advocate for economic education.

While Inside Advocates are needed to promote economic education, even more important is the support of the *Opinion Leaders*. Opinion Leaders are the people who informally influence the opinions of others in the system.[16] To promote economic education, support will be needed from Opinion Leaders on school boards, in parent organizations, on school faculties, and among district

[14]Rogers and Shoemaker, *op. cit.*
[15]*Ibid.*
[16]Turnbull, *op. cit.*

administrators. In identifying Opinion Leaders, it is important to realize that they are not necessarily official leaders or innovative people. Opinion Leaders are considered "one of us" by the group, and they are not likely to deviate much from group norms or to take great risks in trying new things. Where there are several groups or cliques, there is probably an Opinion Leader for each.

One can identify Opinion Leaders by observing who is speaking when others seem most attentive. In-service workshops, school board or P.T.A. meetings, and discussions in teachers' lounges and lunchrooms provide opportunities to observe Opinion Leadership. It is also helpful to ask people whose opinions they respect and consider carefully.

Support from the Opinion Leader is crucial for introducing a new idea. On the other hand, resistance from an Opinion Leader is a barrier that is almost impossible to overcome. For these reasons, it is crucial to identify Opinion Leaders and to consider how the new approach to economic education might appeal to their needs and values. It is equally important to gain the support of Gatekeepers.

Gatekeepers are the people whose official approval is needed to make a change.[17] Whoever must give approval for purchasing new materials, for holding an in-service meeting, or for taking a field trip is an important Gatekeeper if his or her approval is needed to institute a change in economic education.

A good example of involving Gatekeepers can be seen in the D.E.E.P. approach. The superintendent's support is required before a school system undertakes a D.E.E.P. program, and other Gatekeepers serve on key committees during both the planning and implementing stages. This comes from the belief that if a person participates in the design of a curriculum, he or she becomes committed to helping generate resources and providing assistance during implementation.

Gatekeepers, Opinion Leaders, and Inside Advocates are important to the success of economic education programs. D.E.E.P. coordinators, economic education center directors, curriculum supervisors, department heads, teachers, and consultants who want to introduce changes must involve individuals holding those key roles. Introducing a change is, however, only the beginning.

IMPLEMENTING CHANGES

After a new program, approach, or set of new materials in economic education has been initially adopted, it is still necessary to give continued attention to the change to ensure successful implementation. Research has found that training with supporting materials, the principal's support, and "mutual adaptation" are important to the success of new programs.

Training combined with the availability of *materials* is an important factor.[18] Either half of the equation by itself is inadequate. Centers of economic

---

[17]Paul Berman, "Characteristics of Successful In-Service Programs." Paper presented at the annual meeting of the American Educational Research Association, Boston, 1980.

[18]Paul Berman and Melbrey W. McLaughlin, *Federal Programs Supporting Educational Change*, volume VIII (Santa Monica, California: Rand Corporation, 1978).

education have traditionally recognized this. They base their programs on teacher training which includes developing materials that can be used in the teachers' classes. Similarly, D.E.E.P. committees usually plan for in-service training and either the development of materials or local adaptations of materials available through the D.E.E.P. network.

Most of the changes suggested in this Bulletin will require the dual supports of training and available materials.

Because of the high mobility of teachers and frequent changes in teaching assignment, it is important that training be available to people who do not work with the innovation until the second or third year.[19]

The principal's support is another factor that is important after a new program is introduced.[20] If the principal takes a "show me" attitude, teachers will be afraid to take risks with something new; but if the principal gives assurances that he or she is behind the program and understands that there will be initial difficulties to overcome, then teachers will persist with the change. Principals can often make it easier to get over those initial problems by providing consultant assistance, time for teachers to work on the problems, or money to make the change successful. But, most importantly, the principal can set the tone which says we are going to do our best to make this work.

"Mutual adaptation" is the term used to describe the process by which people make changes in an innovation so it will best fit their particular needs. Mutual adaptation is a key to successful implementation.[21] Guidance should be given to teachers in making adaptations so that the value of the innovation is maintained as they adjust it to fit their needs.

Because it is inevitable that difficulties will arise whenever something new is tried, one should plan ahead to provide assistance. Consultants, principal support, and mutual adaptation can all help to overcome those difficulties. An example of this is seen in the D.E.E.P. experiences, where a range of resources is provided for trouble-shooting during the implementation phase. Consultants, D.E.E.P. coordinators, economic education center directors, and specially trained teachers in economic education are all individuals available for helping those having problems in implementing the curriculum. But the best resource for solving problems is usually the teachers themselves. Consistently teachers report that the greatest help to them when they tried something new was the assistance of other teachers in thinking through with them ways to overcome the difficulties as they arose. Teachers' workshops and staff development programs are ideal for this interaction.

Finally, one must realize that new programs which are quite successful are often abandoned simply because the system is concentrating on other priorities. To ensure continued attention to economic education, advocates in the school, in the administration, and in the community must be nurtured.

---

[19]*Ibid.*

[20]Berman, *op. cit.*, 1980.

[21]Sally Schumacher, "Limitations of a Research, Development and Diffusion Strategy in Diffusion." Paper presented at the annual meeting of the National Council for the Social Studies, Boston, 1972; and William Hering, "Some Effects of Change Teams on the Dissemination of New Curricular Materials." Unpublished doctoral dissertation, University of Illinois, 1974.

As readers of this Bulletin make plans to introduce changes in schools to improve students' understanding of economics, we hope they will benefit from the experiences of those who have gone before them. Creating a felt need, emphasizing compatibility with needs and values, reducing perceived complexity, and gaining the support of Inside Advocates, Opinion Leaders, and Gatekeepers is important to the initial adoption of new ideas, practices, and materials. Once introduced, the change must be sustained by training and readily available materials, the support of the principal, and assistance in problem solving and adaptation until the innovation is successful.

It is clear that it takes much time to diagnose carefully the system in which one hopes to initiate a change and to monitor carefully the implementation of that change after it has been made. But the investment in time will pay off in improved, sustained instruction in economics for our youth. Too often in the past our schools have jumped from one fad to another, wasting human energy in the process and not bringing about any improvement. Careful attention to planning for change will protect economic education from that fate.

BIBLIOGRAPHY

Becker, W.R., Jr., J.D. Helmberger, and J.L. Thompson, "An Evaluation of a Developmental Economic Education Project, Given Limited Data," *Journal of Economic Education,* 6:2, Spring, 1975, pp. 120–125.

Berman, Paul, "Characteristics of Successful In-Service Programs." Paper presented at the annual meeting of the American Educational Research Association, Boston, 1980.

Berman, Paul and Melbrey W. McLaughlin, *Federal Programs Supporting Educational Change,* volume VIII, Santa Monica, California: Rand Corporation, 1978.

Dickey, Ouida W. and Joyce B. McAdams, "Planning and Implementing a D.E.E.P. System," *The Georgia Social Science Journal,* volume VIII, 1, Winter, 1977, pp. 9–12.

Hahn, Carole L., "Research on the Diffusion of Social Studies Innovations," in *Review of Research in Social Studies Education: 1970–1975,* Bulletin 49, Washington, D.C.: National Council for the Social Studies, 1977.

Hahn, Carole L., "Attributes and Adoption of New Social Studies Materials," *Theory and Research in Social Education,* March, 1977.

Havelock, Ronald T., *Planning for Innovation Through Dissemination and Utilization of Knowledge.* Ann Arbor: University of Michigan Institute for Social Research, 1969.

Hering, William, "Some Effects of Change Teams on the Dissemination of New Curricular Materials." Unpublished doctoral dissertation, University of Illinois, 1974.

Joint Council on Economic Education, "Developmental Economic Education Program: A Guide for Implementation," 1979.

Marker, Gerald, "Why Schools Abandon New Social Studies Materials," *Theory and Research in Social Education,* March, 1980.

North Carolina Council on Economic Education and the North Carolina Department of Public Instruction, "The Developmental Economic Education Program in North Carolina," 1978.

Rogers, Everett M. and F. Floyd Shoemaker, *Communication of Innovations: A Cross-Cultural Approach.* New York: Free Press, 1971.

Rushing, Francis W., "Promoting Curriculum Change in Economics: A Model," *Southern Social Studies Quarterly,* volume 1, number 2, Winter, 1975, pp. 33-35.

Saylor, J. Galen and W. M. Alexander, *Planning Curriculum for Schools.* New York; Holt, Rinehart and Winston, 1974, pp. 23-27.

Schumacher, Sally, "Limitations of a Research, Development and Diffusion Strategy in Diffusion." Paper presented at the annual meeting of the National Council for the Social Studies, Boston, 1972.

Soper, John C. and Judith Staley Brenneke, "The New Test of Economic Literacy and an Evaluation on the D.E.E.P. System," *Journal of Economic Education,* Summer 1981.

Superka, Douglas, Sharryl Hawke, and Irving Morrissett, "The Current and Future Status of the Social Studies," *Social Education,* volume 44, May, 1980, pp. 36-67.

Symmes, S. Stowell, ed., *Handbook for Curriculum Change.* New York, Joint Council on Economic Education, 1969.

Turnbull, Brenda J., Lorraine I. Thorn, and C. L. Hutchins, *Promising Change in Schools.* San Francisco: Far West Laboratory for Educational Research and Development, 1974.

Walstad, William B. and John C. Soper, "A Model of Economic Learning in the High Schools." Paper presented at the Allied Social Science Association Meeting, Denver, Colorado, September, 1980.

Since the nation cannot pay its hospital bills, we must learn wellness. Since we cannot renew major energy sources, we must practice conservation. Since the supply of fresh water is finite, we must prevent pollution. Since computing, engineering, communications and other technologies are making decisive and determinative impacts on our existence, we must learn how to plan, choose and evaluate. The required curriculum is not in place in our schools.

We need not only intellectual knowledge and appreciation, but the modification of our own habits, behavior and decision-making capacities. The debate on the new questions must go on in the classrooms, in public forums and in the private and personal arena. Action is called for, or crippling results.

John G. Driscoll
President, Iona College

Courtesy of Tom Carter, University of West Florida Information Services

CHAPTER 4

Economic Education: Using the Community As a Learning Resource

MARIANNE W. TALAFUSE AND
DENNIS J. WEIDENAAR

INTRODUCTION

I f any discipline focuses on everyday events, it is economics. Indeed, the great English economist Alfred Marshall defined economics as the study of mankind in the ordinary business of life.[1] Public understanding of economics will be enhanced, then, to the extent that people can improve their perception of the nature and impact of their everyday experiences.

By focusing on everyday experiences as the starting point for understanding economics, we implicitly recognize two important characteristics of economics education. First, this understanding is a lifelong process. It does not begin with that first economics lesson in the social studies class, in which children are taught mechanically to differentiate between producers and consumers. And it does not end upon completion of the senior-high-school economics class, or with the two-semester college course in principles. Second, at the expense of oversimplification, it can be said that understanding economics can be effectively derived through observation and participation in everyday experiences. These experiences are most likely to come from direct contacts within the learner's community.

Although the last statements may appear obvious, they are worth emphasizing because they raise the question: Do the classroom activities used and the curricular materials created to help students of all ages understand economics reflect realistic everyday experiences? For example, the widely used "Trade-offs" series incorporates a number of decision-making vignettes that a typical child presumably confronts at one time or another.[2] These vignettes have been carefully constructed to include the important concepts that comprise decision-making. One popular scenario involves a child making a decision as to

---

[1] Alfred Marshall, *Principles of Economics,* Eighth Edition (New York: Macmillan Company), p. 1.

[2] The "Trade-offs" television/film series is a set of fifteen economics lessons for students between the ages of 9 and 13. The series is based on personal and group decision-making situations. It was developed jointly by the Agency for Instructional Television, the Canadian Foundation for Economic Education, the Joint Council on Economic Education, and a consortium of forty-eight state and provincial agencies, 1978.

which toy to purchase with a limited amount of money. Another describes the conflict a teenager goes through in determining how best to earn money to purchase an automobile. Are these and the hundreds of similar examples that appear in traditional curricular materials faithfully capturing experiences that reflect the daily decisions of children? Do the materials comprise the study of humankind in the ordinary business of life?

It is not our purpose to criticize this series in particular, or economic education curricular materials in general, but rather to suggest that economic educators may have relied too much on traditional vehicles with simulated or unreal examples for helping students to understand economics. Real-life experiences are so vibrant and, by definition, so relevant that it would be a tragedy if such opportunities were not used more than they presently are.

The experiential component of both social studies and economic education is primarily a function of the community environment. The community serves as a life-long teacher and provides an arena in which students can practice the decision-making skills discussed by H. Michael Hartoonian in Chapter 2.

The rest of this chapter describes approaches to economic education that involve use of community resources. These are illustrations of the potential for using the community as learning resources. We have arbitrarily divided the examples into two categories: Classroom-Related Approaches and Approaches Outside the Classroom.

CLASSROOM-RELATED APPROACHES

John W. Muth and Lawrence Senesh have pointed out:

Not long ago, the community played a direct and important part in the education of youth. . . . In the past the schools have been one of the institutions communities looked to for help in dealing with problems. The social studies curriculum has been and should be one important element in this. Unfortunately, the concept-oriented social studies curriculum, as it is taught today, has largely lost contact with real life.[3]

A System-Based Social Science Curriculum

In response to the above perception of social reality, Lawrence Senesh has created a curriculum that uses the community as a laboratory for teaching economics and, indeed, the social sciences.[4] The objective of this program, which is called a System-Based Social Science Curriculum, is "to help to increase the options of youth in their home communities as well as in communities to which they might migrate, and at the same time, to help the young people grow roots in the communities where they might decide to settle."[5]

The focal point of this program is the development of a community social studies profile that becomes a tool for educational decision-makers by providing insight into how forces, both within and outside of the community, affect the well-being of its members. The profile is a written description of the social

[3]John W. Muth and Lawrence Senesh, *Constructing A Community System-Based Social Science Curriculum* (Boulder, Colorado: ERIC Clearinghouse for Social Studies/Social Science Education and Social Science Education Consortium, Inc., 1977), pp. 6 and 7.
[4]This program is summarized in the Muth and Senesh publication cited earlier.
[5]*Ibid.*, p. 1.

system of a community. This description provides information as to how the community functions, how it has changed over time, and what occupational opportunities it provides that assist young people in determining what kind of training they should and can procure; and it helps them to assess the benefits and costs of staying and moving.

The community profile can be prepared in a number of ways. Key resource persons are the social science faculty of the community working with high school juniors and seniors. The schools, in turn, may call on local representatives of agriculture, labor, business, government, and education for information.

Five different dimensions of a community's life are described in the profile. They are the physical environment, history, economic aspects, political structure, and culture of the community. The community social profile includes supplementary materials such as readings, interviews, newspaper articles, and historical documents. The profile can be put to many different uses. Its main use, however, is as an educational decision-making tool within the classroom structure. Through the process of collection, observation, and interpretation of data, students learn how the forces inside and outside a community influence the well-being of its members.

This project was dedicated to the idea that schools serve the people, that the people of a community have the right to shape their own institutions, and that knowledge of the community is necessary in order to make intelligent decisions. As its name implies, the curriculum includes many dimensions in addition to the economic, recognizing that experiences in the real world do not neatly fit the boundary lines of academic disciplines. A specific example of the application of this curriculum is Project *LINKS*, developed in Elkhart, Indiana.[6]

Unit-Based Social Studies Projects[7]

● *A Second-Grade Economics Study* by Dolly M. Pittenger, *Fulbright Primary School, Little Rock, Arkansas*

The project began as a study of endangered animals and expanded to become a totally integrated learning experience in economics, visual arts, poetry, environmental education, career education, politics, language arts, and reading. Economic issues related to endangered animals were used for developing the concepts and their applications. As I developed the goals for the study, I kept in mind John Dewey's philosophy of education. Dewey placed great importance on investigating one's everyday world in a scientific manner. He believed that one learned best when a problem situation was handled in a

---

[6]A description of the Elkhart experience, called Project LINKS, is available from Joseph A. Rueff, Director, Elkhart Community School Corporation, Elkhart, Indiana 46514. He also serves as coordinator of the Developmental Economic Education Program (DEEP) in the Elkhart district.

[7]These brief descriptions are selections from award-winning units of study entered in the 1978-79 and 1979-80 Awards Program for the Teaching of Economics, conducted by the Joint Council on Economic Education under the financial sponsorship of the International Paper Company Foundation. Hundreds of other examples are fully annotated in *Economic Education Experiences of Enterprising Teachers*, now in 18 volumes, and available through the JCEE at nominal cost. Readers may obtain free loan copies of the entries themselves by writing to the National Depository for Economic Education Awards, Milner Library 184, Illinois State University, Normal, Illinois 61761.

rational manner and appropriate problem-solving techniques were used to formulate goals, weigh the existing evidence, examine alternatives, and arrive at some objective conclusion.

As the project unfolded, the children were given the opportunity to interact freely and cooperatively with each other. Many occasions arose which required the pupils to make important decisions. The children were encouraged to set their own goals, organize their resources, and investigate ways of bringing about change in our society.

After reviewing the basic economic ideas, the children were then introduced to a study of endangered animals. We took a field trip to the zoo, read stories about animals and prepared posters of animals classified as endangered or extinct. Resource people were invited into the classroom to keep the students' interest high and help them understand that the basic problem of scarcity confronts all individuals. The children were surprised to learn how much money it cost to operate and maintain a zoo.

A speaker from the City Parks Commission, Herbert Hoover, discussed the Zoo of Arkansas's master building plan and the politically volatile issue of an admission fee for the zoo. Although Mr. Hoover was obviously in favor of a zoo admission fee as a fund-raising device, many of the children were not immediately convinced of its value. One pupil wrote, "I don't think the zoo should charge an admission fee because it wouldn't be fair to poor people." This situation made the students think more about the costs of operating a zoo and the sources of revenue required to support the annual budget of nearly one-half million dollars. The students were amazed at the number of choices and trade-offs involved in the zoo's budget-making decisions. They discovered that well over half of the zoo's budget went to pay salaries and that inflation and higher energy costs also had an effect on the zoo's budget. Sources of revenue for the zoo included federal matching funds, state support, donations, a zoo admission fee, or revenue bonds. The pupils were led to understand that planning the annual budget required taking into account inflation, cost estimates of machinery to be replaced, major repairs to be completed, wages and salaries for employees, acquiring new animals, the zoo's utility bills, and other fixed costs.

● *A Third-Grade Unit* by Berna Jo Gaylor, *C. H. Decker Elementary School, Las Vegas, Nevada*

The project was designed to help students understand the relationship between government and the economic system. "The SUN Audits the IRS," an article in the local newspaper, stimulated the children's interest and helped launch the study. In one activity, Lieutenant Governor Myron Levitt visited the class and explained the major issues and problems related to the MX missile site proposed for the state of Nevada. *The First Book of Local Government* was used to explain the purpose and function of both city and county governments. Posters and bulletin boards were prepared to illustrate important facts and information about the federal government, including how a bill becomes a law. Films, filmstrips, and posters were used to help students understand that government provides many goods and services and that there is a continuing and as yet unresolved debate concerning the role of government in the U.S. economy. A film, *Nevada and Its Resources,* led to a discussion of productive resources, of the problem of scarcity and the ways the state used its limited resources to produce goods and services. Students conducted surveys to find out what local citizens thought were the most important goods and services government at all levels could provide. Evaluation results indicated that the children increased their understanding of basic economic concepts and practices.

● *A Fifth-Grade Economics Unit* by Dorris Reed Morris and George P. Nickle, Jr., *Warner Elementary School, Wilmington, Delaware*

Our school has a magnificent location on a bluff overlooking the Brandywine River, the original power source for the E. I. Du Pont Company as well as many other companies. As we looked at the river, an idea began to form. Why not study the economic importance of the Brandywine? After all, the river was there, the old waterwheels were there, so why not put them all to good use? As the waterwheels turned, so did the economic development of eighteenth and nineteenth century Wilmington.

Of our 160 students, 80 percent come by bus from places at least twelve miles away. The remainder of the students are city residents who walk to school. We discovered that neither group knew very much, if anything, about Wilmington or the Brandywine. Wilmington and the Brandywine therefore became our richest sources of information and inspiration for the project. Learning about them became the common denominator for us, our common bond, and a seemingly inexhaustible source of this year's economic education experiences.

Activities were many and varied. We were able to use old and new maps, build and study working models of mills and waterwheels, and talk with local historians. We walked through the city, sketched it, and learned to appreciate it. We also began to realize why there is now such a proud rebirth of interest in renovating or remodeling older sections of Wilmington. We were visited by the mayor and met other city officials, such as city council members. In short, the city and the Brandywine became extensions of our classrooms.

In addition to studying the economic history of the Brandywine, we also involved the children personally in economic decision-making by creating a simulated society called "Tiny Town." Tiny Town was in operation for nearly the entire school year and its effectiveness was greatly enhanced by the use of the *Trade-Offs* economic education television series. Our study of the Brandywine River, which ran for three months, became an interesting and rewarding companion to Tiny Town. Each was an educational complement for the other.

The students found it exciting to realize that primary source material about the Brandywine River existed, dating back to 1783. They had learned about the use of primary resource material from their social studies basic text, the *Holt Data-Bank System*. That series emphasizes the idea that historical evidence is necessary to back up inferences.

The primary source material we used was a collection of descriptive accounts about the Brandywine River, the flour mills, the initial interest of E. I. Du Pont and his purchase of the land, and a walking interview through the powder yards, compiled in 1890. Each describes impressions and observations by the various authors. We also used many photographs from the Eleuthere Mills-Hagley Foundation Collection.

In addition to these materials we used Du Pont Company work and salary records from 1870 to the present, U.S. Census data dating back to 1870, and reproductions of Sears catalogues, starting in 1897. These materials all gave a realistic quality to our study, and were a source of accurate (and surprising) information to our students.

Our studies had two general goals. First, we wanted students to discover what life was like in Brandywine Village in the late eighteenth and nineteenth centuries. Second, it was important to help pupils understand why the community developed as it did, and what was being done to preserve the remaining structures and recapture the atmosphere of the early town. We hoped that the study of the economic growth, history, and restoration of an area using a familiar and nearby setting would help make the past fresh and alive for the students and give them an appreciation of what's going on there today.

● *A Junior High School Unit* by Richard A. Aieta, *Hamilton-Wenham Regional High School, Beverly, Massachusetts*

The project focuses on the economics of the port of Gloucester and the impact of the 200-mile-limit law on the fishing industry centered there. Students study a nearby community and obtain information about its resources in order to develop relationships between concepts taught in the classroom and the real economic world. The first phase of the experience is essentially teacher-directed as students become familiar with the intent and impact of the 200-mile-limit fishing law, which went into the effect in 1976, and reactions to it. Students read a specially prepared booklet, listen to taped interviews, and use news clippings and government reports to build a data base. Students then go on a field trip to Gloucester to gather firsthand and primary source information by participating in conducted tours. Organized in groups of four or five, the students interview resource people who had been previously contacted. Back in their classrooms, the students put the two phases of the program together and write an essay on "The Economics of the Fishing Industry," in which they link economic concepts they studied with their experiences in Gloucester. The unit is divided into four parts and takes thirty-one days: (1) data collection about the Gloucester economy and the 200-mile-limit law — 10 days; (2) preparation for the field trip to Gloucester (tours, organization, interview techniques, etc.) — 5 days; (3) field trip to Gloucester — 1 day; and (4) analysis of the Gloucester economy — 15 days. The project emphasizes the utilization of community resources and includes taped interviews with members of government regulatory bodies, economists, bankers, biologists, fishermen, executives of fishing companies, and conservationists.

● *A Junior High School Unit* by Anna E. Mayans, *Xavier University, Cincinnati, Ohio*

The unit focuses on the specific needs of the students at Sawyer Junior High School, a predominantly black, inner-city school. The two-year program, entitled "Making Choices," was completed by a committee composed of junior high teachers under my direction. Preliminary surveys were taken by the committee to ascertain the students' knowledge of economics; their preference ordering of specified skills; and their home backgrounds, interests, and needs. The content of the unit was determined on the basis of the information gathered from the surveys, a previous determination of the economic concepts basic to an understanding of personal choices and decision-making, and the amount of school time available (in this case one quarter to ten weeks). Four basic questions were emphasized: (1) Why do we make choices? (concepts of scarcity, opportunity costs, etc.) (2) What do we use to make choices? (money, credit, banks, etc.) (3) How can we make better choices? (consumer economics, career education) and (4) What affects our choices? (supply, demand, price, market, etc.) Practical application of the concepts presented included learning about the opportunity costs of a decision; taking field trips to a local bank and local manufacturer to learn about their functions in the economy; filling out job applications, resumes, credit and social security forms; role-playing job interviews; learning about advantages and disadvantages of paying in cash or charging credit; learning where to borrow money; and comparison shopping. Of particular use in the program were school alumni who served as resource speakers. Although the unit is not intended to provide a comprehensive understanding of economics and the U.S. economy, it does serve to provide valuable experiences to the students in making choices and decisions in their daily lives.

● *A Senior High School Unit* by David E. O'Conner, *Edwin O. Smith School, Storrs, Connecticut*

The unit, "The Economics of Energy," used the case-study approach as part of an elective course called "Economic Understanding," open to eleventh- and twelfth-graders. The unit, designed to cover twenty-three periods, stressed the following eight concepts as they relate to the production and consumption of energy: scarcity and choice-making, supply and demand, economic wants, externalities, productive resources, opportunity cost and trade-offs, government intervention, and growth. Students assumed active roles in assessing the current energy crisis and investigated alternative proposals for alleviating it. Students became involved with all aspects of approach as they applied basic concepts to new "real-life" issues. Over the duration of the unit, students were engaged in the production of a variety of materials which were later used by their classmates to define issues and to develop parameters of the study. Included among the student productions were collages, a class magazine, a scrapbook, and a videotape and slide presentation. All led to discussion, debate, and questioning. Presentations by local resource persons and a class trip to the Millstone Nuclear Power Plant also contributed to the realism needed in the case approach. Students learned about a variety of energy sources and saw that the value of the study extended beyond the four walls of their classroom.

● *A Senior High School Unit* by John Joseph Kerrigan, *Chicago Public Schools, Center for Economics and Business Studies*

During the second semester of the 1976-77 school year, a Center for Economics and Business Studies was established to develop an exciting experiment in alternative education. The center was cosponsored by the Continental Bank and the Chicago Board of Education.

The curriculum was designed to teach students economics, personal finance and planning, consumer education, and business organization while familiarizing them with Chicago's business and financial community and the career opportunities it offers. In particular, the money cycle, including money creation, the role of the commercial banking system, and the function of the Federal Reserve System were explored in depth.

In conducting their research on Chicago and its resources, the students met key persons representing the business community, labor organizations, and government agencies. Through individual and team activities, students became familiar with the city's financial district and the uniqueness of Chicago as a cultural and educational center.

In the program that was developed, the teacher relinquished his traditional role as the center of the learning experience. Instead, individualized learning was promoted through the utilization of community resources. For example, as part of the orientation, students toured Continental Bank, including the main building and check-processing facilities, and met with key personnel. The class was given a walking tour of the financial district, including a visit to places of business and cultural interest.

In dealing with union-management relations, the class was divided into two negotiating teams representing the Widget Company and the International Brotherhood of Widget Workers. The two teams were coached by representatives from management and labor in a collective bargaining simulation. After several negotiating sessions, the parties could either agree to a contract, declare an impasse, or submit to third-party intervention. At the National Labor Relations Board, the class investigated the role of that organization under the National Labor Relations Act.

Economic decision-making and its accompanying concepts were utilized to aid the students in determining possible career choices. The use of career days and career inventories also aided in this process. Through an analysis of manpower statistics, reflecting both levels of employment and wages for certain industries and careers, the class became acquainted with the present labor force situation. Wage determination was treated in terms of traditional wage theories (marginal productivity) as well as by evaluation systems utilized by industry. A representative from Chicago United discussed levels and types of unemployment (structural, cyclical, and seasonal) that are found in Chicago and the different programs developed to meet unemployment problems.

APPROACHES OUTSIDE OF THE CLASSROOM

During the 1970s, the potential for a new outreach in adult economic education appeared within the framework of employee economic education activities.

Employee Economic Education Programs[8]

Three basic types of programs have emerged, although their characteristics overlap in numerous ways.[9] The first kind of program can be identified as focusing on academic economics as opposed to consumer economics or business economics. It can be characterized as a mini-principles of economics course. Basic economic concepts such as supply, demand, elasticity, monetary theory, and macroeconomics compose the curriculum. The classroom format is generally used, and the presumption is made by the developers and sponsors of the program that these concepts will be taught in such a way that they are "exciting and relevant" to the employee.[10]

The second type of program deals with business economics issues; that is, an examination of the peculiar economic problems and decisions that the employing firm confronts in its activities as a producer. In the context of dealing with these business problems, it is necessary to stress numerous economic concepts; and, therefore, this approach provides a forum for economic education. This type of employee economic program has one overwhelming appeal. Most employees are, at best, lukewarm in their enthusiasm for learning academic economics; but they are eager to learn more about the decisions made by their companies, and, of course, about the impact that those decisions have on their own lives.[11]

The third type of program usually is described as a Summer Intern Program for Professional Teachers. It is one in which career teachers are selected and "inducted" into the actual everyday experiences of a business firm for as long as ten weeks in the summer. The purpose is to help teachers and, in turn, their students relate more effectively to the everyday experiences of work.[12]

Economic understanding, while traditionally regarded as the responsibility of the schools, is now augmented, in some cases with significant resources, by the private sector. Numerous economic educators have been called upon to

---

[8]The most comprehensive summary and evaluation of employee economic education programs is found in *Corporate Economic Education Programs: An Evaluation and Appraisal,* by Myron Emmanuel, et al., 1979. It is a research study prepared for the Financial Executives Research Foundation (33 Third Avenue, New York, New York 10017).

[9]There are activities conducted by some businesses which have been falsely marketed under the name of economic education. Actually, these programs are designed explicitly to increase the participant's appreciation for free enterprise and to involve the employees in pursuing political action on specific issues that is favorable to the company. We do not regard such programs as economic education.

[10]An example of a program fitting this model is the one designed for and sponsored by TRW Incorporated, Cleveland, Ohio. The goal of this program is to raise employees' awareness of the fact that, in a world of scarce resources, every choice has a cost and that cost is measured in terms of the real resources that must be given up to achieve the benefits of that choice.

[11]The Sperry Rand Corporation program exemplifies this approach. Its objective is to inform its employees about the business system and how it applies to their company and jobs.

[12]Corporations such as Quaker Oats, General Motors, Borg-Warner, and Ingersol-Rand are conducting such programs.

assist businesses in developing such programs. Such calls for assistance provide both an opportunity and a challenge. Economic educators gain the opportunity to interact with a segment of the population with which they normally have little contact, and the opportunity to provide employees with appropriate economic understanding to improve their decision-making skills as consumers, producers, and voters. At the same time, however, there is a challenge to economic educators to provide an objective presentation of basic economic understandings, noting carefully, where possible, the fine line of values, both in terms of content selection and presentation mode.

Community Agencies and Associations

This section includes a number of examples of how diverse community agencies can provide a framework within which the everyday activities of life can be highlighted.[13]

Educational Organizations.   Recently ten programs on "The Economic Facts of Life: Living With Less" were presented to the Missouri Division of the American Association of University Women. The programs were concerned with public policy governing the production, distribution, and consumption of food which is scarce relative to world demand, and with the questions of values that determine choices among many alternative courses of action. The program format provided a forum for speakers from the humanities, economics, and a broad spectrum of farm, labor, and business leaders interested in economic education. Each program allowed for discussion by the members of the audience as they engaged in dialogue with the speakers. At the conclusion of the discussion, groups formulated policy statements, and communication was initiated with state legislators on the farm issues. Examination of the human values involved in economic choices was the central point of each program. The programs were evaluated by a count and study of the communications made to legislators and by a follow-up, both from and to state lawmakers.[14]

Cultural Organizations.   A computer-assisted exhibit at the Indianapolis Children's Museum is designed to increase visitors' understanding of the economic concepts of scarcity, trade-offs, and opportunity costs, through the medium of four microcomputer simulations: *Kingdom, Sell Robots, Star Trader,* and *Carnival.* In *Kingdom,* the visitor is declared the ruler of the kingdom of Malthusia for three years. As the ruler, he or she must make difficult decisions concerning the creation and allocation of resources. *Sell Robots* is designed to teach the concepts of supply and demand and equilibrium price. *Star Trader* creates a space-like environment of dramatic graphics and sound effects in which to convey the economic concepts of scarcity, choice, trade-offs,

[13]In addition to the agencies and institutions cited in relation to specific economic education activities, a comprehensive listing of agencies that might be used is provided in the *Encyclopedia of Associations,* edited by Nancy Yakes and Denise Akey, 13th edition, Volume 1 (National Organization of the United States, 1979).

[14]The programs were funded by a grant from the Missouri Committee for the Humanities, Incorporated. Each state has such a committee funded by the National Endowment for the Humanities.

and opportunity costs. *Carnival* is designed to teach the concept of profit.

The simulations indicate what choices are available and the consequences of specific choices. Evaluation reveals that this method of economic education is appealing to children and promotes rational decision-making based on economic concepts.

Chambers of Commerce.   An active committee of most local Chambers of Commerce is the Education Committee. Committee members recognize that everyone is a consumer, producer, investor, and citizen. Based on the perception that the study of economics helps people to make choices which maximize their limited resources of time, energy, and money, Chambers of Commerce encourage, with both financial and human resources, the development of workshops for teachers and other community leaders.

Most frequently, the model emphasizes experiential economics representing specific areas of interaction with the economy presented by local Chamber of Commerce members. Ordinarily, the workshop director plans activities with the chairperson of the Education Committee; and the Education Committee provides panel members, respondents, and speakers.

The workshop director is responsible for the objectivity of such workshops through the choice of content and speakers from labor, government, and agriculture, as well as speakers from the business community and academic world. Teachers and other community leaders attending such workshops become aware of local community resources, including speakers, field trips, and materials. The utilization of such resources increases as a result of the increased awareness.

Agricultural Organizations.   The Indiana Farm Bureau, Inc., annually sponsors a "Young People's Citizen Seminar." Approximately 150 high school juniors and seniors spend a week studying the purpose, function, structure, and organization of political parties, county governments, and state lawmaking. A major session is devoted to economic education. It may include a lecture, game, film, or a combination of these things. After games or films, debriefing sessions link economic decisions to political decisions.

Religious Organizations.   Religious organizations, such as the Newman Foundation and the Economic Foundation for the Clergy, work with economic educators to plan and present workshops to groups such as campus ministers. "The Economic Order and Religious Values" was sponsored recently by the National Institute for Campus Ministries, Indiana Newman Foundation, Indiana Council for Economic Education, and Economic Education Foundation for the Clergy. It featured a diversity of economic and moral viewpoints and allowed ample opportunity for discussion by participants.

The staff included economic educators, industrial leaders, union representatives, and a theologian-in-residence. The workshop was designed to provide analytical tools to interpret and evaluate the economic world and to present opportunities for interactions between campus ministers, economists, and representatives of business, labor, agriculture, and government. Such workshops provide opportunities for reactions to current economic issues and problems, and responses that may be based on religious beliefs.

CONCLUSION

Everyone experiences economics from the time of birth to the time of death. Before children begin their formal education, they confront scarcity and the necessity for economizing as members of families. These real-life experiences are a powerful learning tool and increase in richness as the child's world is extended into the classroom. If the economic education taught in the school-room is assimilated with out-of-school life, students will leave the classroom with an understanding of what it means to be proficient consumers, producers, and citizens.

Upon conclusion of their formal education, young adults become full-time participants in the marketplace, continuing their life-long experiences as consumers, producers, and citizens. When a community and its schools are fused into one continuous learning laboratory, the ordinary business of life becomes the basis for extraordinary economics education.

What we need is an ecological balance between those potentially educative institutions that could do much more educating than they now do and an institution, the school, that carries an exclusively educational function. The line between education and training, between preparing for what is and preparing for what might be, would be less important for the nonschool institutions. However, such a line would be critical for schools. Schools would concentrate solely on the "knowledge, attitudes, values, skills, and sensibilities" that require for their cultivation in the individual "deliberate, systematic, and sustained effort."

John I. Goodlad
Dean, Graduate School of Education
University of California, Los Angeles

Courtesy of Cathy Schober, Louisiana Council on Economic Education

Evaluating Student Learning of Economics: Investment-Good and Consumer-Good Rationales

WILLIAM E. BECKER AND WILLIAM B. WALSTAD

Testing students for comparative evaluation purposes remains a major topic of debate among educators. On the one hand, parents want to know how Susie or Johnny is doing in school, and society wants to know how well schools are teaching students. Testing may provide quantitative answers to these questions. On the other hand, testing for evaluation purposes is often rejected because of the poor quality of test instruments, or the desire to protect students and teachers from situations of stress. In spite of the debate, testing has spread to all areas of the social studies, including economics. In fact, the Advertising Council, Inc., recently popularized the need for testing in economic education with its mass media query, "What is your E.Q. [economics quotient]?"

Unfortunately, in all the questioning and debate, few educators have examined economic rationales for evaluation in economic education, or other subjects.[1] This chapter develops both an investment-good and a consumer-good rationale for evaluation in economic education. The first section presents the case for standardized testing in economics when economic education is viewed as an investment good. It also describes the practical and technical factors to consider in selecting and using a standardized test in economics. The second section explains the rationale for testing from a consumer-good perspective and gives special attention to the development of classroom tests.

ECONOMIC EDUCATION AS AN INVESTMENT GOOD

In economics, an investment is any act that creates wealth (or capital) and results in additional future income. Since education in economics or other subjects imparts new skills or knowledge, it potentially increases human capital.

---

[1]For a review of current issues that psychometricians and educators consider important in social studies testing, see Moore and Williams. The issues identified by Moore and Williams focus on the content, type, and construction of the test to be given.

The Case for Standardized Testing

Education in economics will give rise to a future societal income stream as long as this human capital is valued in the marketplace by society. If the educational process also identifies more knowledgeable and skilled individuals, then this income stream can be captured by the individual recipient of the education. Of course, there are many nonmarket benefits which can accrue to society and individuals as a result of investment in human capital. For example, more effective economic decision-making may raise the quality of life of individuals and may also raise the quality of life of society.

The identification or screening function of education can involve a single ranking of individuals within a subject area or involve a matching of individuals with tasks for which their knowledge gives them a relative advantage. Either form of screening necessitates the use of standardized tests; without standardized testing, comparisons could never be made outside of a small sample group. In addition, the net benefit to society from either form of screening can vary and, thus, the intended use of standardized tests should be carefully considered.

The Use of Standardized Tests for Student Ranking

To see the results of a screening process in which individuals are simply ranked by their score on a standardized test, consider a situation developed by Becker (1977), where the population consists of individuals who can be described by a single characteristic — achievement. Let this characteristic be proportional to an individual's productivity — i.e., his or her income-generating ability. However, individuals of higher achievement can receive a higher income only if they can be identified as being more productive than the individuals of lower achievement.

While individuals may know their own achievement, the market does not, in the absence of any information. The market treats all individuals equally. That is, in the absence of identification, possible employers could not distinguish among individuals on the basis of their academic achievement and future productivity. In such a world all individuals would receive an income equal to the mean value of the population. Such would be the case, for instance, where everyone graduates from high school with no grades or distinguishing marks.[2]

If testing takes place, however, those labelled high achievers would receive an income higher than the average, while low achievers would receive an income lower than the average for the population as a whole. Thus, high achievers would desire screening if the difference between their income and the mean income for the population exceeds the cost of screening. It can be demon-

---

[2]In this world of undistinguished students, the mean income which every graduate would receive can be calculated by the formula:

$$\overline{W} = \frac{p(A_H H + A_L L)}{H + L}$$

Where W equals income (and is proportional to achievement), H equals the number of high-achievement individuals in the population, L equals the number of low-ability individuals, A equals achievement, and p is the productivity coefficient that relates achievement to income.

strated that under these conditions, with screening, the gross gain in income to a high achiever may exceed the loss to a low achiever. Society as a whole, however, would be worse off by the screening if the achievement levels themselves are not affected.[3]

By contrast, if the act of ranking individuals on the basis of test scores caused some individuals to increase their achievement levels, then society as a whole, as well as motivated individuals, would benefit. Becker (1982) has shown that increased screening will generate motivational effects, at least for the high-achievers. These motivational effects may be so strong that society will benefit even if low-achievers do not respond to more screening. When standardized tests are administered for the intent of ranking student achievement, social and private gains will be made if the cost of preparing and administering the test is offset by the motivational effect on high achievers.

Ranking students on standardized tests within the classroom or within the school district may not only lead to increased learning by students, but also serve as the means for assessing the student progress and evaluating the educational process. Positive motivational effects can be expected if society (i.e., the market) values this ranking information. Furthermore, comparisons over time, or comparisons between groups at a point in time, are made possible through the use of standardized tests. A pretest performance, for example, can be compared with a posttest performance to find out if students showed any gain in general economic understanding during an instructional unit. Or student posttest performance can be compared to the norming sample of students for that grade level to determine whether students are doing better or worse than the comparison group.

Instructional decisions can also be made by using the ranking obtained from standardized test data. Pretest data can be analyzed to find out what economic concepts students know and what concepts should be stressed during a course. A mid-course administration of a test can be conducted to obtain information indicating whether instructional strategies need to be changed. The pretest/posttest comparison data can be used as feedback to the teacher in an evaluation of the instructional unit. But, as will be pointed out later, such use of tests need not be related to viewing education as an investment good.

---

[3]For example, if $H = 25$ people, $L = 75$ people, $A_H = 200$ points, $A_L = 100$ points, $W_H = \$200$, $W_L = \$100$, and $p = \$1$ (one achievement point is worth $1 in increased income), then

$$\overline{W} = (\$1)\frac{(200)\ (25)\ +\ (100)\ (75)}{100} = \$125$$

If testing of all 100 individuals costs $1,500, then the individuals who know they are the higher achievers will gladly pay for testing while low achievers will only pay if required by law. For the time being, assume no such law and that higher achievers are willing to pay $60 a person to be tested ($1500 ÷ 25). As a result of the school's screening function, the market (possible employers) knows those who are more productive. Each more able individual gains $15 ($200 − $60 − $125), for a total gain of $375 (25 × $15). The private return to education for these individuals is clearly positive. However, each lower achiever has a loss of $25 ($125 − $100), for a total group loss of $1,875 (75 × $25). The net social return to testing is thus negative, since the population as a whole lost $1,500 ($1,875 − $375).

The Use of Standardized Tests for Identifying Comparative Advantage

If testing is viewed as an inexpensive means of assisting students in establishing comparative advantages, then such screening is clearly providing a productive function to society. In this case, testing is providing a positive "externality" in the form of information. To illustrate, assume that there are two types of output produced by society, each valued at $1.00 per unit, and two kinds of individuals. Individuals of characteristic A_x can each produce 100 units of output X and zero units of output Y. Individuals of characteristic A_y can each produce 100 units of output Y and zero units of output X. If the size of the population is 100, with 50 of each type of individual, then random assignments of jobs would imply an output for society (GNP) of $5,000. On the average, half of society would be in the wrong occupation. With equal income distribution, however, all individuals share in the output, with each individual receiving $50.

If testing can screen individuals by assisting them in finding their most productive jobs at a cost of less than $5,000, then society and individuals can gain from screening. With perfect screening, the 50 people who have a comparative advantage in producing X would be identified. Similarly, the 50 people who have a comparative advantage in producing Y would be known. Society could thus produce 5,000 units of X and 5,000 units of Y. At a testing cost of $1,000, for instance, society's net GNP would be $9,000. All individuals would be in their most productive occupation. With the cost of education allotted equally and with equal income distribution, each individual would receive $90. The private and social return to testing is clearly positive for this type of screening.[4]

To provide maximum social benefit from standardized tests as a means of assisting students in identifying their comparative strengths, it would be necessary to have standardized tests at all grade levels and in all subjects. Then, a student could compare his or her ranking in one subject versus another subject and easily establish his or her comparative advantage. However, tests are not always available for all subject areas or grade levels, and tests are imperfect measures of student achievement. While these problems may reduce the maximum social benefit from standardized testing, the allocative benefits from testing can still be substantial.

Selecting a Standardized Economics Test

After understanding the investment rationale for test selection, one is faced with the problem of locating a standardized test that can be used for ranking students and assisting them in finding their comparative advantage. In economics, in contrast to the other social studies subjects, standardized tests are available at most grade levels.[5]

---

[4]For example, assume that the 25 high achievers in the above example increase their individual achievement levels on the test from 200 points to 300 points, as a result of the motivational effect of knowing that their achievement will be recognized and rewarded. Now each high achiever gains $115 over the situation of no screening ($300 − $60 − $125). The total gain to society is $2,875 (25 × $115). In this case, the motivational effect of ranking students on the basis of test scores causes the net social return to testing to be positive; the population as a whole gains $1,000 ($2,875 − $1,875).

[5]For a listing of social studies tests, see Needham (1981).

For students in grades two and three, there is the *Primary Test of Economic Understanding* (PTEU). At the intermediate elementary grades, the new *Basic Economics Test* (BET) replaces the outdated *Test of Elementary Economics* (TEE). The *Junior High School Test of Economics* (JHSTE), as the name implies, can be administered at the seventh- through ninth-grade levels. Senior high school students in grades eleven and twelve can be tested with the new *Test of Economic Literacy* (TEL), which is a substantive revision of the old *Test of Economic Understanding* (TEU). Finally, for those teachers of advanced courses or advanced students at the high school level, the revised *Test of Understanding of College Economics* is available in microeconomic, macroeconomic, and hybrid versions.[6]

Among other practical considerations in using standardized tests—and one of the most important—is *cost*. School budgets are limited, and the cost of testing needs to be kept at reasonable levels. Fortunately, twenty-five reusable copies of any of the above economics tests with a test manual costs only about nine dollars. Also, the cost of scoring can be very low, since a sample scoring key for teachers is provided in the test manual.

Ease of administration is another basic consideration for teachers. The multiple-choice format of the tests and the clear directions printed in the test manual make testing a simple procedure for both teachers and students. The test length and time period for testing also appear to be optimal; most students can easily complete each item of the test in a normal forty- or fifty-minute class period.

Finally, a teacher needs to analyze the characteristics of the class and the testing situation before using a standardized test. The reading ability of the students, the level of test anxiety, the time of year of testing, and a host of other factors can cause testing problems. A test that is given on a day before a holiday, for example, may not provide a true indication of students' knowledge of economics. Using a standardized test to evaluate student learning from a specialized teaching unit on "Third World Countries" and to assign grades may be seen as another example of inappropriate test use, because the unit may cover only a limited number of economic concepts found in the standardized test. Only a teacher can judge whether a class is suited for standardized testing and when the conditions are right for the administration of a test.

Technical Characteristics of a Test

Standardized tests in economics exhibit rather desirable technical properties. The validity, reliability, and norming features of a standardized test can be used to judge the quality of a test for comparison purposes.

Content Validity. The first property is content validity, or the degree to which items on a test adequately represent the subject of economics. If an

---

[6]A Test of Understanding of Personal Economics (TUPE) is currently available, but it needs revision. References for the PTEU (Davison and Kilgore), BET (Chizmar and Halinski), TEL (Soper), and TUCE (Saunders) are in the bibliography of this chapter. The Education Testing Service also has a 90-minute, 100-item, multiple-choice economics test which is part of its College Level Examination Program. Because of its high cost and tight security regulations, it has been used in few research studies. See, for example, Siegfried.

economics test contained only questions about international trade, the test would not be considered a valid measure of general economic understanding, since much of the content of economics would not be assessed by test items. Thus, a good economics achievement test includes a representative sample of test items covering major economic concepts or topics, if the test is to possess content validity.

Establishing content validity is a complex process and essentially involves a series of rational judgments by experts in economics and education. The development of the new *Test of Economic Literacy* (TEL) can serve as a brief illustration of the process of validating content. For the TEL, the *Master Curriculum Guide for Teaching Economics in the Nation's Schools, Part I—A Framework for Teaching Economic Basic Concepts* (MCG) was used to define the content categories for economics. The MCG was written by a respected group of economists and represented the most current statement of important elements necessary for general economic understanding.

A valid economics achievement test not only covers the subject matter, but also contains test items which assess students' understanding at different cognitive levels. The cognitive levels may range from knowledge, where answering a question simply involves students' use of memory, to evaluation, where answering the question requires students to make judgments based on accepted standards. A modified form of Bloom's *Taxonomy* was used to define cognitive levels for the TEL. When the cognitive categories are combined with the economic content categories, a test specification matrix is produced, as shown for the TEL Form A in Table 1 (pages 59-60).

Using the test matrix as a guide to content and cognitive-level coverage, a working committee of economics and education experts developed sample test questions, which were reviewed, revised, and field-tested. Those items showing a medium difficulty level, the power to discriminate between students of high and low levels of economic understanding, and a suitable readability level for the age of the group tested were retained in the final test. Each instrument was also reviewed by a national committee of economists and educators to serve as a final check on the content validity of the test.

Reliability.   The second important property for an economics achievement test is reliability, or the capacity of the test to measure student performance accurately. This quality of a test is critical because an instrument which measures student economics learning with too much error cannot be used for making comparisons or decisions. While no test perfectly measures student performance, it is the degree of consistency or reliability that is important.

In contrast to judgmental procedures for determining content validity, reliability is evaluated with reference to statistical estimates.[7] Good reliability coefficients for standardized achievement tests range from .70 to .90 (1.00 would be a test with no error). The TEL has a reliability estimate of .87 for both forms of the test.

---

[7]Reliability can be estimated a number of ways (i.e., Kuder-Richardson 20, Cronbach Alpha). For the specific meaning of a type of reliability estimate, consult a test and measurement text.

TABLE 1: Content Categories for the TEL	Cognitive Level
A. The Basic Economic Problem	**I** Knowledge
1 Economic wants	
2 Productive resources	
3 Scarcity and choices	
4 Opportunity costs and trade-offs	**II**
5 Marginalism and equilibrium	Comprehension
B. Economic Systems	
6 Nature and types of economic systems	
7 Economic incentives	**III**
8 Specialization, comparative advantage, and the division of labor	Application
9 Voluntary exchange	
10 Interdependence	
11 Government intervention and regulation	**IV** Analysis
C. Microeconomics: Resource Allocation and Income Distribution	
12 Markets, supply and demand	
13 The price mechanism	
14 Competition and market structure	**V**
15 "Market failures": information costs, resource immobility, externalities, etc.	Evaluation
16 Income distribution and government redistribution	

D. Macroeconomics: Economic Stability and Growth

(Table 1 continues on page 60)

17 Aggregate supply and productive capacity
18 Aggregate demand: unemployment and inflation
19 Real and money income; price level changes
20 Money and monetary policy
21 Fiscal policy: taxes, expenditures, and transfers
22 Economic growth
23 Saving, investment, and productivity

E. The World Economy

24 International economics

F. Economic Institutions

G. Concepts for Evaluating Economic Actions and Policies

Economic goals: freedom, economic efficiency, equity, security, price stability, full employment, and growth
Trade-offs among goals

Overall Specifications for the TEL *(continued from p. 59)*

Content Categories	Form A					No. of Questions	Per Cent
	Cognitive Categories						
	I	II	III	IV	V		
A 1							
2		1					
3		2					
4			3				
5			19			4	8.7
B 6	4	6					
7	5						
8		7					
9			8				
10							
11			9			6	13.0
C 12		11	14,15				
13			16,17	22			
14		12	20,21				
15		13			23,24		
16	10			18		14	30.4
D 17		33					
18	25			38,39			
19	26,30			27,28	42		
20	31,32	34					
21			37	40,41			37.0
22		35					
23		36				17	
E 24		43				1	2.2
F	44,46					2	4.3
G					29,45	2	4.3
Total number of questions	10	12	11		5	46	100.0
Per cent	21.7	26.1	23.9	17.4	10.9	100	

NOTE: The entries in the matrix cells are the question numbers in the TEL.

An alternative measure of reliability and one more useful for the teacher is the standard error of measurement (SEM). The SEM provides an estimate of the amount of error or variation that can be expected in a student's test score. In fact, the SEM statistic suggests that a student's test score is probably best considered as lying within a range of possible test scores. For example, a raw score of 25 on the TEL, which has a SEM of 3.0, means that a teacher could be

67 percent certain that a student's true test score is between 22 and 28 (25 ± 3.0). A teacher would be 95 percent certain that the true test score is between 19 and 31 (25 ± (2 × 3.0)).[8]

Norming.   The third major property of an economics achievement test is the availability of national norms or standards. Norms are useful for converting a raw score to a percentile rank and making a comparison to a larger sample of the population at that age level. If an eleventh-grade student without economics instruction received a raw score of 25 on the TEL, then a teacher could interpret the raw score as meaning that the student scored as well or better than 75 percent of the norming sample of eleventh graders without economics instruction.

Norms are developed using a cross-section of the population at that age level. The TEL norms were established from data obtained in 92 classes in different regions, different metropolitan areas, and schools of different sizes. Although this norming sample may not be completely representative of all eleventh- or twelfth-grade students, the norming sample begins to approximate the larger populations. However, when using norms, teachers need to keep in mind that comparing a student's performance against the norm sample is not exactly the same as comparing a student's performance against all students at that age level. Also, the older a test is, the greater the probability that the norms are outdated; and test experts believe a standardized test needs to be revised or renormed after, at most, fifteen years. Most of the economics tests are still usable according to this criterion, but a few tests are showing their age.[9]

ECONOMIC EDUCATION AS A CONSUMER GOOD

Classroom or teacher-made tests in economics differ substantially from standardized achievement tests. Generally, the test is developed by the teacher, rather than a committee of economics and education experts. The test content area is often more limited and based on the objectives of a particular teaching unit or school curriculum. Test items are not pretested, and little is known about test reliability. The test is usually administered to one class, and no opportunity is available for comparison of test results with a larger norming sample. As such, it is difficult to justify their use based on the investment criteria.

The Case for Classroom Tests

While the classroom test lacks the known technical qualities of the standardized test, the classroom test can be justified when education is viewed as a consumer good. If the purpose of testing is to determine whether specific curriculum objectives in economics have been met, then the classroom test can

---

[8]The imprecise nature of testing is often cited as reason for not carrying out evaluation. Only through the use of standardized tests can this inaccuracy be specified. Becker (1980) has shown that as the precision of measurement increases, at least high achievers will increase their desire to achieve more.

[9]For more information, the JHSTE and PTEU are reviewed in Buros. The BET was normed in 1978, the TEL in 1977, the JHSTE in 1973, and the PTEU in 1971.

demonstrate to the consumer (the student and his or her parents) that the promised product was delivered. That is, the classroom test can be used by the teacher to provide feedback to the student on the fulfillment of the instructional unit objectives.

Unlike the purchase of an ice cream cone, the educational process by itself provides no visible sign of service rendered. Results of a classroom test can provide that visible sign. If all the instructional objectives for a unit are specified at the onset, a student's results on a classroom test, which is tied to those objectives, may demonstrate the successful completion of that unit. This consumer-good rationale is the basic idea behind competency-based education. The student contracts for a given outcome, and passing the classroom test demonstrated the delivery of that product. In business terms, "all sales are final upon delivery."

Practical Considerations for Teacher Test Construction

Since the classroom test measures the delivery of an educational product, the careful construction of a test becomes most important for ensuring the accuracy of measurement. A detailed discussion of the steps in test construction is beyond the scope of this chapter, and more explanation can be found in a number of sources (Helburn; Morris and Fitz-Gibbon; Sax). A few "rules of thumb," however, should help to outline the test construction process.

The first step in building a classroom test in economics is for the teacher to specify clearly the goals or objectives for the unit. For example, if a class is involved in an experiential problem-solving unit on production, where students are actually making goods to sell, then one behavioral objective might be stated as follows: "Students, after completing this unit, should be able to identify the three factors of production (land, labor, and capital) in different examples of production processes." Each unit objective should be tied to specific student behavior, and the list of course objectives should cover the range of learning experiences found in the unit.

Once the important course objectives are identified, then the second stage of the test construction process begins—the development of the test plan. From each objective, a list of economic concepts or content topics is made. In the example given above, the "factors of production" would be added to the list of economic concepts tested. The test plan or test matrix combines the content areas or concepts with cognitive categories to specify the domain for test-item construction, similar to Table 1. Weights can be placed on those concepts or content areas where a teacher considers it to be especially important to develop test items.

The third step of test construction involves writing the items. Here, the teacher first has to decide whether items are to have a fixed response, as in the case of multiple-choice, true-false, or matching questions, or an open response, as exemplified by short-answer or essay questions. There are obvious advantages and disadvantages to each test format. The fixed response type is easier to grade and allows the teacher to sample more of the test matrix than the essay or short-answer test. On the other hand, the essay or short-answer test is easier to construct and can often tap higher cognitive skill levels than the fixed-response test. Ultimately, the teacher will have to choose the format, and, again, specific references on developing essay questions or multiple-choice questions should be consulted.

After selecting the format for the test items and writing a set of questions, the teacher should select the best test items for inclusion in the final fixed or open response test. Attention should be given to whether the test items cover the major areas of the test matrix and whether sufficient weight is given to those content areas stressed during the instructional unit. Other considerations include setting an appropriate time limit for the test, establishing the length of the test, and determining the level of difficulty of test items. If possible, a review of the test by other teachers would help identify any weak or confusing test items.

Administering and scoring the test is a fairly standard procedure for most teachers, but a few points deserve special emphasis. The teacher can help students prepare for a test by identifying in advance the basic test objectives, major features of the test plan, and the format for test items. Scoring the test can be simple for the fixed-response type test, but developing a systematic and objective scoring procedure for essay or short-answer tests is difficult. With the essay test, it is best for the teacher to develop a score key for major points that will be given credit. Several readings of the same essay question for all students should enable the teacher to determine the distribution of scores based on appropriate responses listed in the score key.

The final part of developing a good classroom test is the posttest analysis of results. Although few teachers have the time to make a detailed analysis, the feedback from an analysis can aid a teacher in pinpointing weaknesses in unit instruction and in building better tests. The analysis can be conducted using the total test scores for the class or using individual responses to test items. The total distribution of the test scores will give some indication of the overall difficulty of the test, while analysis of individual items will identify poor test questions.

Classroom tests in economics are important to teachers for providing periodic evaluation of students' learning from instructional units. Creating a good classroom test takes work, and it is no wonder that many teachers turn to textbook tests or build up test files to make the process easier. No matter what test is used, it needs to be analyzed after each administration to obtain information about the performance of students and to judge the quality of the test instrument.

CONCLUSION

Evaluation of students' learning of economics is desired if economic education is viewed as either an investment good or consumer good. When economic education is considered as an investment good, standardized testing should be used. Society and high achievers will benefit if the results of these tests can be used by students and society to identify comparative advantages. Although it may not be possible to test students' strengths in all subjects, the mere act of knowing their relative position on the national norm from an economics test will cause high achievers to increase their desire to achieve in economics. If the cost of testing is low and the gains in achievement are high, then society will realize a net benefit from standardized testing.

The consumer-good perspective on economic education requires a simpler type of evaluation. In this case, the job of the teacher is simply to document whether the instructional objectives of economic education have been achieved. The documentation can be done with paper-and-pencil classroom tests, or, alternatively, individual and group techniques can be used by a teacher to overcome some of the limitations of paper-and-pencil testing.[10] Students, for example, can be interviewed by the teacher to find out their ability to identify basic economic concepts taught in a unit and the application of those concepts to novel situations. If a classroom unit involves the production of something, then the final product can serve as an artifact or record of group activity. Also, teacher-written observations or records of group work in the production process can supplement the artifact evidence. In other words, alternative ways exist to obtain evidence of student learning without resorting solely to objective classroom tests. These alternatives may not be very useful for measuring relative achievement, as is necessary if economic education is viewed as an investment good; but the information can provide teachers with supplementary evidence to document classroom learning missed in paper-and-pencil evaluations.

BIBLIOGRAPHY

Becker, William E., "The Educational Process and Student Achievement Given Uncertainty in Measurement," *American Economic Review* (Forthcoming March 1982).

Becker, William E., "Investment in Human Capital," in Warren G. Meyer, *Vocational Education and The Nation's Economy.* Washington, D.C.: American Vocational Association, 1977, pp. 59-76.

Bloom, Benjamin S., ed., *Taxonomy of Educational Objectives: The Classification of Educational Goals,* Handbook 1: Cognitive Domain. New York: David McKay Co., 1956.

Brown, Frederick G., *Principles of Educational and Psychological Testing.* Hinsdale, Illinois: Dryden Press, 1970.

Buros, Oscar Kristen, ed., *The Eighth Mental Measurement Yearbook,* Volume 3. Highland Park, New Jersey: Gryphon Press, 1978.

Chizmar, John F. and Ronald S. Halinski, *Basic Economics Test Examiner's Manual.* New York: Joint Council on Economic Education, 1980.

---

[10]For other examples of subjective type evaluation, see Ellis and Alleman-Brooks, or Sax, pp. 397-505.

Davison, Donald G. and John H. Kilgore, *Primary Test of Economic Understanding Examiner's Manual.* Iowa City, Iowa: College of Business Administration, The University of Iowa, 1971.

Ebel, Robert L., *Essentials of Educational Measurement.* Englewood Cliffs, New Jersey: Prentice-Hall, 1972.

Ellis, Arthur and Janet Alleman-Brooks, "How to Evaluate Problem-Solving-Oriented Social Studies," *The Social Studies,* 68:3, May/June 1979, pp. 99-103.

Hansen, W. Lee, G.L. Bach, James D. Calderwood, and Phillip Saunders, *Part I; A Framework for Teaching Economics: Basic Concepts.* Master Curriculum Guide in Economics for the Nation's Schools. New York: Joint Council on Economic Education, 1977.

Helburn, Suzanne Wiggins, "How to Develop Your Own Social Studies Tests in Economics," *Social Education,* November/December 1976, pp. 533-537.

Junior High School Test of Economics Interpretive Manual and Rationale. New York: Joint Council on Economic Education, 1974.

Moore, Jerry R. and Paul L. Williams, "Social Studies Testing: Current Issues," in *Criterion-Referenced Testing for the Social Studies.* Washington, D.C.: National Council for the Social Studies, 1980.

Morris, Lynn Lyons and Carol T. Fitz-Gibbon, *How to Measure Achievement.* Beverly Hills, California: Sage Publication, 1978.

Needham, Richard, "Bibliography of Social Studies Tests," in *Criterion-Referenced Testing for the Social Studies.* Washington, D.C.: National Council for the Social Studies, 1980.

Saunders, Phillip, *Revised Test of Understanding in College Economics: Interpretive Manual.* New York: Joint Council on Economic Education, 1981.

Sax, Gilbert, *Principles of Educational Measurement and Evaluation.* Belmont, California: Wadsworth, 1974.

Siegfried, John J., "Is Teaching the Best Way to Learn?" An Evaluation of the Benefits and Costs to Undergraduate Student Proctors in Elementary Economics, *Southern Economic Journal,* January 1977, pp. 1394-1400.

Soper, John C., *Test of Economic Literacy: Discussion Guide and Rationale.* New York: Joint Council on Economic Education, 1979.

Test of Understanding in Personal Economics: Interpretive Manual and Discussion Guide. New York: Joint Council on Economic Education, 1971.

While working with children I came to the conclusion that content and methodology are two sides of the same coin. They are inseparable. Each dimension reinforces the other, and economic educators should possess competence in both areas.

Lawrence Senesh
Professor of Economics
University of Colorado

Courtesy of Center for Economic Education Northern Michigan University

CHAPTER 6

Teacher Education: The Continuous Process

ELMER D. WILLIAMS

For many years, economics has been a largely neglected content area in teacher preparation programs. Recent developments, however, seem to bode well for the future of economic education in our nation's schools and colleges.

It is becoming increasingly clear that the nation's schools are caught up in a "back to basics" movement. A critical public, often faced with increased taxation to support its schools, has begun to demand that schooling result in citizens with certain "basic" knowledge, skills, and abilities. In many cases, the result has been a rather narrow definition of "basic," with increased emphasis on reading, mathematics, and other curriculum areas in which basic knowledge and skills are somewhat agreed upon by educators and can be communicated fairly clearly to the public. This is not to deny the importance of these areas of the curriculum; for without the ability to read, write, and perform elementary computational skills, many students would be unable to function effectively in other areas of the school curriculum. However, in the initial clamor to ensure that students can read, write, and compute, programs of social studies, science, and humanities have often been de-emphasized or neglected, resulting in what many educators would describe as undesirable balances in the overall school curriculum.

It is entirely likely that this has come about not because the public views social studies as non-essential — a "frill" of the curriculum — but because social studies educators have been less successful than the proponents of other subject areas in explaining to a worried public just what is "basic" or essential about social studies in helping students to lead productive lives. In light of the rather conflicting views within the profession as to the goals of the social studies, it is not surprising that there is lack of agreement as to what is "basic."

One outcome of the "back to basics" movement has been the trend toward defining and, in some cases, mandating minimum competency standards. Conflicting data are found concerning the number of states actually mandating minimum competency standards for elementary and secondary students. Pipho (1978, pp. 585-8) reports that as of March, 1978, thirty-three states had taken some action to mandate the setting of minimum competencies, with all the remaining states having either legislation pending or state board studies underway. Moore and Williams (1980) present data which suggest that the minimum competency movement may not be that pervasive. Less than 50% of the state social studies supervisors responding in the Moore and Williams study reported that their state mandated graduation competencies in one or more areas of the curriculum. Whatever the actual number of states requiring minimum competency standards, however, the trend has been established and is likely to accelerate.

In the area of social studies, Moore and Williams found that thirteen states have specific graduation competency requirements. Another eleven states were reported to be likely to require such competencies in social studies in the near future. These authors indicate that the results of their study suggest that minimum competencies are best characterized as mandated subjects, rather than as mandated curriculum goals and performances. A much larger number of states—thirty-eight—were reported to have required social studies courses. The most commonly required courses include American history, state history, government, and economics.

Further illustrating the growing influence of economics in the social studies curriculum, Frye (1979), in an examination of statewide mandates in economic education, found seventeen states mandating the teaching of economics, with another three states considering such a mandate. In twelve states the mandate is legislative; the other five states have Board of Education mandates. Eleven of the mandates require the teaching of economics at the secondary school level; six states have K-12 mandates. In approximately half of the states, the mandate takes the form of a specific course in the social studies curriculum. With the exception of only two states, these mandates are products of the 1970s.

Goals stated in the mandates fall into four major categories: (a) to help students become more capable consumers and producers, (b) to improve students' ability to make economic decisions, (c) to improve students' understanding of the world in which they live, and (d) to teach about free enterprise. It may surprise many readers to learn that only five states specifically identify the teaching of free enterprise as the goal of their mandate. The vast majority of the mandates have goals which appear to reflect the belief that students need to be better equipped as producers, consumers, and citizens, with an understanding of the world around them, including a positive understanding of the American economic system.

Economics instruction takes place in other states besides those mandating the teaching of this discipline. State boards of education may recommend the teaching of economics at various grade levels; economics may be required at the secondary level by local school systems; secondary teachers integrate economics into many other courses of the social studies curriculum; and early childhood, elementary, and middle-school teachers infuse economics into all subjects of the school curriculum in many novel ways. Indeed, interest in the teaching of economics—whether it is mandated or not—is growing nationally at a steady pace. Textbook publishers rate the market conditions for instructional materials in economics as better than in any other secondary social studies courses or topics. Publishers' ratings of the importance of economic content at the elementary level also point out the subject's growing influence on the social studies curriculum (Schneider and VanSickle, 1979).

Literally thousands of teachers are either teaching courses in economics or integrating economic content into their social studies programs. Effective classroom implementation requires teachers who are equipped with an adequate conceptual background in subjects that they are to teach and a knowledge of appropriate instructional materials. How well are these teachers trained to deal with economic content? What do state boards of education require for a teacher of economics? What efforts are colleges and universities expending in order to educate teachers in economic education?

Frye (1979) reported that ten of the seventeen states requiring the teaching of economics do not require that teachers take any economics courses for certification. The other seven mandating states generally require only one or two courses in economics. In no state was in-service training in economic content or the use of new materials mandatory, although some local districts do make such a requirement. Very few non-mandating states require any economics for their secondary teachers; the general pattern is to require a certain number of hours in the social sciences, including courses in two or more of the disciplines. At the early childhood and middle-school levels, even fewer states require their teachers to have academic background in economics. While requirements for certification to teach in any subject area are determined by state boards of education, college and university teacher education programs generally attempt to prepare teachers to meet those certification requirements. However, in the absence of specific certification requirements, it would be atypical for a college or university to require an economics course of its undergraduate teacher education majors in social studies or elementary education. Thus, as a rule, one will find little or no economics in the preparation of most prospective teachers. Considerably more activity in economic education takes place in graduate or in-service teacher education programs, where teachers—often personally aware of the divergence between their academic background and what they are expected to teach or would like to teach—have opportunities to participate in a wide range of educational experiences. But even at this more advanced level of the profession, a relatively small proportion of teachers has received any training in economics and/or economic education. The combined result of all of our efforts in economics for teachers is that half of all social studies teachers have never taken an economics course and even fewer of the rest have taken more than one (Wakin, 1980).

TEACHER EDUCATION IN ECONOMICS

Traditionally, the model of economic education for teachers has been one of a discipline-centered organization based on the university-level course commonly entitled "Principles of Economics." Discipline-centered instruction is based on the logical organization of those concepts that comprise the discipline of economics. Most university economists — and university economists do conduct a major share of teachers' economic education — have already ingrained in them a mind-set based on this discipline-centered organization of instruction. While this model may be appropriate in some circumstances, teachers' instructional mind-sets often do not match this method of organization. Indeed, many teachers, especially those not teaching a specific course in economics, have probably never seriously considered organizing their teaching on a structure of the disciplines model.

The purposes of this section are to describe three alternative models adapted from Townshend-Zellner (1977) for organizing economics instruction for teachers, and to present sample pre-service and in-service economic education programs for teachers that are illustrative of these models.

Alternative Models

Topic, Unit, or Issue Centered Instruction.   Most social studies teachers do not teach specific courses in economics; rather, their instructional programs include topics, units, or issues with significant economic implications. In this model, the teacher education program focuses on the topic, unit, or issue to be taught by teachers, with economic concepts in a subordinate role to the actual subject matter being covered. Economic concepts are taught only as they are needed to explain or give meaning to the topic being taught. Teachers are not expected to master a large body of economic content, but instead employ specific economic concepts as tools with which to analyze or enrich the topic of study.

For example, instruction for elementary teachers might focus on such traditional curriculum topics as families, communities, or regions of the world. An excellent example of instruction so organized is found in the publication *Master Curriculum Guide in Economics for the Nation's Schools: Part II, Strategies for Teaching Economics, Primary Level* (1977). Many elementary teachers include a unit on the home community or city in their instruction, and an interesting economic experience might be constructed around this topic. At the secondary level, the emphasis might be on the issues and topics contained in an American government course, or popular topics such as environmental contamination, sexism, and ethnicity, which are increasingly being included in social studies curricula. Again, in this model, the economics taught to teachers would be only that needed to give meaning to the topics, units, or issues around which classroom organization is frequently organized.

Curriculum Materials Centered Instruction.   In situations where a specific economic education material, or set of materials, is of high quality and highly motivating and involves extensive treatment of economic concepts, it may be productive to organize instruction for teachers around it. In this model, the material itself becomes the organizational core, with economic concepts used primarily to explain and enrich the material and its use in appropriate subjects, topics, or units.

Organizing instruction around materials can be highly cost-effective. For example, over 15,000 copies of a comprehensive materials kit, "Teaching Economics in American History," produced by the Joint Council on Economic Education, has been distributed nationwide to middle and secondary school teachers. Numerous short-term workshops were conducted to introduce the material to teachers. If each kit were used by a teacher for one year with four classes of twenty-five students each, the per pupil cost of the materials, based on a cost of thirty dollars per kit, was approximately thirty cents. Use of the materials in subsequent years was zero cents per pupil. When compared to the cost of typical textbooks, this alternative is obviously very attractive to many school administrators.

Examples of other curriculum materials around which teacher education has been focused are the Mini-Society elementary materials developed by Kourilsky (1974) and the highly popular, upper elementary/middle school television series "Trade-offs" (1978).

Economic Concept Centered Instruction.   In some cases, perhaps most noticeably at the elementary level, economic concepts may be appropriate as the organizing basis for educating teachers. Typical organizing concepts of the elementary social studies curriculum might include such basic concepts as scarcity, specialization, producer/consumer, etc. Even at the secondary-school level, some economic concepts, such as inflation, unemployment, and the world economy, may be so prevalent in the social studies curriculum as to make instruction for teachers based on those specific concepts justifiable.

Pre-Service Teacher Education in Economics

Undoubtedly, the weakest link in economic education is at the pre-service level. While numerous workshops, courses, and other types of educational experiences are conducted for practicing teachers, very few institutions of higher education offer anything like these opportunities for prospective teachers. Most teachers of social studies, including some who teach economics courses, enter the profession with a non-existent, or, at best, very limited knowledge of economics. As noted earlier, many states which have mandated the teaching of economics at the pre-collegiate level do not even require any economics training as a prerequisite for teacher certification.

Early Childhood and Elementary Education.   Although a basic course in economics has frequently been recommended for elementary school teachers (*College Preparation for Teaching Economics,* 1969), the reality of the matter is that most teacher education programs in early childhood/elementary education include a few required courses in social science, such as American history, with the rest of the social science curriculum being composed of a few electives. This is not necessarily undesirable, but the result, without excellent faculty advising, may be students taking courses having little or no relationship to what they will eventually be teaching in their first school. On most college campuses, one would find very few elementary education students with an economics course on their transcripts. A notable exception to this pattern is found in the state of Arkansas, long recognized as a leader in economic education, where the course "Economics for Elementary Teachers" is required for certification. Although economics and education professors teaching this course might follow very different models, the reader interested in examining an elementary education economics course based around the "Trade-offs" curriculum materials is encouraged to obtain a complimentary copy of the publication "Trading-off for Trade-offs" (Clayton, 1979).

With few exceptions, such as that described above, the few prospective elementary or early childhood teachers who do take a course in economics have probably experienced the traditional "Introduction to Economics" course, which is typically organized on the structure of the discipline model. Unfortunately, this course would not acquaint them with available instructional materials, nor would it have as one of its objectives helping students comprehend the potential role of economics in the elementary social studies curriculum.

Middle and Secondary School Education.   A larger proportion of students preparing to teach social studies in middle and secondary schools will complete at least one economics course in their collegiate program. However, a significant number will not take any economics, and many of those will not have studied the subject during their secondary school years. Should an economics course be required of prospective middle and secondary school social studies teachers? Given the mandating of the teaching of economics in many states, the growing frequency of such economics-related courses as consumer education and career education being offered in middle and secondary schools, and the strong relationship of economics to many of the other social science courses taught at these levels, the answer, in this writer's opinion, is affirmative. To suggest the requirement of more than one course for *all* middle- and secondary-social studies teachers may be desirable, but is probably also wishful thinking. For the teacher preparing to specialize in the teaching of economics, it is obvious that considerably more than one introductory course is needed.

However, even for the social studies teacher specializing in another discipline—e.g., American history—and taking only one required course, problems are likely to persist. While a basic course in economics such as "Principles of Economics" or "Introduction to Economics," in most cases organized on the structure of the discipline model, would begin to give social studies teachers a conceptual knowledge of the discipline, much more may be needed. Will such a course be a straightforward study of a large number of economic concepts or will selected concepts be taught and then applied to the analysis of contemporary economic problems and issues? Will this course introduce students to available instructional materials? Would the student completing an introductory course be knowledgeable about evaluation instruments useful in determining students' academic achievement? Will this course help students determine which of the multitude of economic concepts are most appropriate for middle- or secondary-school students? Will students, at the very least, be taught by a good model of the effective teaching of economics?

An introductory course is not apt to provide all of the instruction implied by these questions. Where will social studies teachers, very few of whom will specialize in economics or ever take more than one course, obtain these additional inputs? Indeed, will even the undergraduate student specializing in the teaching of economics and taking several courses, perhaps a minor in the discipline, come to grips with these important pedagogical considerations in most departments of economics?

Social Studies Methods Courses.   Much can be done in social studies methods courses to further prepare teachers of all grade levels to deal competently with economics in the classroom. Professors of social studies education with some knowledge of the discipline will find many ways to integrate economics into common topics or units of their methods classes. Demonstrations of methodologies can utilize significant economic content, economic education materials can be analyzed by students, and the development of teaching plans using economic concepts and issues can be encouraged. The list of means by which economics can be used as an exemplar in the methods class can go on and on. Unfortunately, such an enumeration may have little meaning, for college and university social studies educators have had less than two courses of college-level economics, on the average; and about one-fifth have never had a single economics course. Half of those who have had an economics course took the course over twelve years ago. In addition, younger social studies educators, on the average, have taken fewer economics courses than have their older colleagues (Weidenaar, 1977). Given this lack of study of economics in their own academic background, many social studies educators may not feel comfortable using economic concepts and materials in social studies methods courses.

In an effort to ameliorate this problem, the Purdue Center for Economic Education, with financing from the Sears Roebuck Foundation, has offered institutes in economic education for college and university professors of social studies methods. Approximately eighty educators from major public and private institutions of higher education across the country have learned effective ways to integrate economics into their methods courses through this experience. Many have since become intensively involved in a variety of professional economic education programs. For the many others who will not have the opportunity to take part in such a program, the publication *Master Curriculum Guide in Economics for the Nation's Schools: Part II, Strategies for Teaching Economics, The Social Studies Methods Course* (forthcoming), developed by the participants of the Purdue institutes, should prove to be of valuable assistance.

In-Service Teacher Education

In-service economic education presents a much more promising picture. In its 1979 annual report, the Joint Council on Economic Education reported a total of 724 programs, with over 33,000 attendees, conducted by its affiliated network of state councils and college and university centers for economic education. Numerous other offerings were sponsored by other economic education organizations, some by specific business enterprises. For either the teacher who has not taken economics at the undergraduate level and wishes to become informed about the subject, or the teacher who wishes to take specialized, topical courses or learn about methods and materials for teaching economics, opportunities are abundant.

These economic education programs take many forms: from summer workshops to academic year institutes, from those awarding graduate-level credit to those offering staff development credits, from traditional on-campus classroom experiences to internships in businesses, from workshops of a few hours duration to multi-year, system-wide projects attempting to infuse economics in the entire K-12 curriculum, such as DEEP (discussed in Chapter 2). Research does tend to support the contention that students' performance on tests of economic understanding improve significantly when their teachers have participated in in-service economic education programs (Highsmith, 1974).

An examination of post-baccalaureate offerings in economic education by colleges and universities throughout the country illustrates that many of these programs, unlike most undergraduate courses based on the structure of the discipline model, are organized on the basis of the alternative models described earlier. While it is true that a program may not be based on only one organizing model, the program titles listed below strongly suggest the organizers' frames of reference.

Discipline Centered
    Economic Institutions
    Economic Concepts for Elementary Teachers
    Advanced Economic Analysis and Policies
    Principles of Economics

Concept Centered
    Economics of Inflation
    The Transnational Corporation
    Government Taxing and Spending
    Teaching about Productivity

Topic, Unit, or Issue Centered
    Institute in International Trade
    Economics of Nuclear Energy
    The Montana Economy Workshop
    The Economic Dimension of American History
    Personal Investing Workshop

Curriculum Materials Centered
    World of Work Economic Education Program
    Kinder-Economy Workshop
    Dollars and Cents: Economics for Primaries
    You're the Banker

GUIDELINES FOR ORGANIZING
TEACHERS' ECONOMIC EDUCATION

Heretofore, this chapter has presented illustrations of pre-service and in-service teacher programs in economic education and has shown how they fit organizational models. A major disadvantage of each of the models discussed is that it focuses on only one aspect of instruction in organizing educational experiences. In reality, the effective planner does not have a single focus, but considers elements of each of the models in the organization process. The structure of the discipline and its key concepts, how those concepts can be integrated into the topics, units, and issues which will actually be taught to learners, and appropriate instructional materials are equally important components of the planning of *every* educational program in economics. In addition, two significant considerations not addressed in the other models, but very important in the minds of teachers, must be examined. First, experiences of an economic education program must make sense to educators in terms of the psychology of learning and instructional strategies presented in professional education courses. Second, teachers are always searching for specific "how-to-do-it-tomorrow" ideas. A large number of innovative teaching techniques which can be applied later to other areas of the school curriculum can be demonstrated in a well planned course or workshop. While these latter two elements will be of more value to practicing teachers, their serious consideration by college professors will do much to prevent a common complaint from undergraduate teacher education majors: "I just don't see how I can use much of that course when I start teaching." What is being called for is a better integration of the best of economics and professional education. Thus, a comprehensive organizational model should consider each of the following:
- the important concepts of the discipline to be addressed
- topics, units, and issues that teachers will use in presenting the concepts
- classroom instructional materials which the teachers will use
- the instructional strategy; e.g., concept formation, values clarification or analysis, inquiry, etc. being used to teach the concepts
- specific teaching techniques to be demonstrated.

To illustrate how these five components might be considered in just one session or experience of a program, the following example is presented.

An Example—The Federal Budget Lesson

The person utilizing this lesson is teaching in an in-service workshop composed primarily of secondary political science and American history teachers. An initial discussion with the group on the first day of the workshop revealed that (1) many of the teachers deal with the *topic* of government taxation and spending in various courses they teach, and (2) the administration of the school system in which the workshop is being taught has "strongly encouraged" all teachers of the system to integrate more *values education* activities into their courses. The instructor of the workshop decides to use the material (handout)

Figure 1—**Federal Budget Exercise**

Suppose the U.S. Congress was faced with the decision to allocate $100,000,000 for new domestic programs. How would you recommend that the money be spent?

1. Food stamps for poor Americans
2. Research on a cure for cancer
3. Programs for reducing unemployment
4. Expanded health care coverage for the elderly
5. Research and development of new sources of energy
6. Housing for low-income families
7. Grants to local and state governments for crime prevention and control
8. Grants to local governments for education needs
9. Preventive medical services for the poor

Rank the above-mentioned nine items in order according to your priorities; that is, indicate which program you would give the highest priority, which the lowest priority, etc.

Rank Program No.

Highest Priority   1. _____

                          2. _____

                          3. _____

                          4. _____

                          5. _____

                          6. _____

                          7. _____

                          8. _____

Lowest Priority   9. _____

Focus for discussion: By S. Stowell Symmes, Director of Curriculum, Joint Council on Economic Education, 1212 Avenue of the Americas, New York, NY 10036. From *A Resource Guide for Analyzing Health Care Policy*, EPS Series, JCEE, 1977.

shown in Figure 1, rather than an already well developed lecture, to teach the important economic concept of *opportunity cost.*

After providing introductory information on the magnitude of the present federal budget and raising a few questions concerning how decisions on the expenditure of federal monies are made, the instructor asks participants to read and complete the handout. While the teachers are working on the exercise, the instructor tapes nine sheets of construction paper, marked 1-9, along a classroom wall. A few minutes are spent discussing the wide range of responses concerning the program given the highest priority, with participants being encouraged to give a rationale for their choices.

One participant is asked to explain what he "gave up" when he decided to spend the $100 million on housing for low-income families. He responds, "The chance to use the money on all the other programs." With the aid of a couple of clarifying questions, the participant quickly understands that the money could not be spent on all the other programs and that what was actually "given up" was the opportunity to use the money for expanded health care coverage for the elderly, the participant's second priority. Other participants are asked to respond to what they "gave up," and it becomes clear that the group understands that what is given up is the next best alternative for expenditure of the money. The instructor introduces the term "opportunity cost," and participants develop a definition, which is then written on the chalkboard.

When asked to explain why they gave priority to the nine domestic programs in different ways, participants explained that, obviously, "people placed a different importance, or value, on each of the nine alternatives." During a discussion which explored the factors that might account for these differences, one teacher asks, "What are the marked papers on the wall for?" The discussion concludes somewhat abruptly, and the instructor asks participants to stand in a line in front of the number of the alternative which was their highest priority. In a few moments the wide range of responses becomes visually apparent to the teachers. One teacher is interested in her colleagues' ranking of the cancer research program. The group then uses the numbers on the wall to represent the ranking they gave that specific alternative. Again, diversity marks the group's responses, and individuals standing at extremes of the continuum are asked to explain their reasoning. After examining a few more individual requests, the instructor asks each person to stand again in front of the number of the program of his or her highest ranking. The group is asked to take note of the size of the line in front of each number, and the number of people selecting each alternative spending proposal is written directly on the numbered sheets. The teachers then return to their seats.

In debriefing the lesson, the instructor explains that many secondary students still have difficulty when asked to develop a graph or comprehend information presented in graphic form. The technique of developing "human graphs" is presented as one specific idea for helping students to understand the graphing process. The teachers, who seemed to be enthusiastic about this ranking technique for examining one's values, are asked to think of other times in their courses when this strategy might be appropriate. The instructor concludes by explaining that time will be allowed tomorrow for the sharing of participants' ideas about using this technique in their courses, and that during the course of the in-service program many other *techniques* for examining individual and societal values will be presented.

The instructor described in the above scenario has obviously thought about more than the economic concepts to be taught, the materials to be used, and the topics teachers might be addressing in the planning and organization of this workshop. An awareness of instructional strategies commonly used or expected of teachers and knowledge of a variety of specific teaching techniques for implementing those strategies seem to be a part of this person's repertoire. Methodically planning for the inclusion of each of these five components in each experience of an economic education program for teachers will do much to make the program more meaningful to teachers.

Some Additional Considerations

Developing a sound economic education experience at either the pre-service or in-service level is not a simple task. Whether the experience is a three-hour workshop or a four-week intensive institute, a number of additional considerations must be examined by the program organizer. What are the goals of the program? For what audience is the program intended? How will potential participants be informed of the offering? What resources must be arranged? How will the experience be evaluated to determine if the goals have been achieved? These are only a few of the questions asked by an effective planner. Indeed, it is not uncommon for the planning of a good program to consume as many hours of labor as the actual conduct of the experience. The following brief suggestions may be of assistance to educators involved in the organization of economic education programs for teachers:

Conceptual Guidelines

- Concentrate on a few key concepts appropriate for potential use by the target audience. Teach a few selected concepts well and in depth, as opposed to "covering the waterfront."

- Present the economy and economic actions and policies from the viewpoint of different sectors and different "actors." The role of women and ethnic groups in the economy should not be overlooked. Knowledgeable speakers from business, labor, and government help teachers see economic policies and issues from a variety of perspectives.

- Emphasize the use of economic analysis in making decisions about significant economic problems. The use of decision-making models, such as that presented in the "Trade-offs" series or those presented in H. Michael Hartoonian's chapter in this Bulletin, are especially helpful in preparing teachers and students to use a rational decision-making process when analyzing personal and social economic problems.

- Encourage participants to examine the implications of economic actions and policies from a global perspective. In an increasingly interdependent world, teachers and their students must be cognizant of the far-reaching effects of most economic decisions.

Methodological Guidelines

- Arrange a rich bank of instructional resources for participant examination and use.

- Involve participants in the setting of personal and group goals, the daily operation of the program, and the evaluation process.

- Orient instruction to what teachers might be expected to do in their own classrooms. Use successful teachers from past programs to model how they have transferred their learnings to their social studies curriculum.

- Make provision for the differing values and viewpoints of participants. Allow ample time for discussion and make it clear that each person's contributions will be respected.

- Tailor economic content to the needs of the participants. Pretesting will be helpful to both participants and the program planner in determining what should be taught. Ask participants to delineate what they feel will be most appropriate, given their individual teaching situations.

- Have the experience result in a tangible product immediately useful to participants. This final product can take many forms, ranging from one lesson plan to an entire instructional unit, from a listing of commercially available instructional aids to a teacher-developed simulation game. Be sure that adequate time is allowed for the successful completion of teacher products.

- Schedule individual activities in such a way that intake and output sessions are finely balanced, that intense, quiet endeavors are followed by opportunities for group interactions, etc.

LOOKING AHEAD

Although economic education is becoming a part of the academic background of an increasingly larger proportion of prospective and practicing teachers, much remains to be accomplished. Especially important is the need for more professional interaction between economists and social studies education professors. Educators need to know more about the discipline of economics; economists must become more knowledgeable about major instructional strategies and teaching techniques recommended by education professors. Economic education programs for teachers must demonstrate the best of what is known in economics *and* education. The five-component organization model presented in this chapter strongly suggests that effective program planners must be masters of both disciplines if their endeavors are to result in meaningful experiences for classroom teachers. Perhaps, through more cooperative ventures, such as the team teaching of courses and workshops, the economist and educator can learn from each other.

A critical reexamination of the role of economic education in the academic training of undergraduate teacher education majors is also necessary. Can a nation which prides itself on the sophistication of its educational system be satisfied with the prospect of beginning teachers instructing its youth in content areas in which they have no formal training? What disciplines should be required in the social science curriculum for prospective teachers? Do the present social science requirements, many of which were determined years ago, adequately prepare teachers for social studies instruction in the classrooms of today and tomorrow? What will be the response of teacher education institutions to the mandating of the teaching of economics at the pre-collegiate level? If these institutions see no need for a formal requirement in economics, will their faculties encourage teacher education students to take elective courses in economics? These are all important questions for the faculties of our colleges and universities which prepare teachers.

Given the lack of economic education in the training of beginning teachers, the present number of social studies teachers with little knowledge of economics, and the "drop out" rate in the profession after about five years of experience, there will be a continual demand for introductory programs in economic education. The challenge is for us to make these "first exposures" to economics the best experiences possible.

Those teachers who do remain in the profession may experience the "burn out" phenomenon and may require economic education programs quite unlike the majority of those offered in the past. The emphasis in economic education will most likely begin to shift toward more specialized, topical courses for teachers who will have already participated in other economic education programs. College credit for advanced degrees may no longer be a powerful incentive; the new incentive may well be what "survival skills" the program will offer; that is, what the program will present that is immediately usable in the classroom. Programs of the 1980s will need to take into account the potential role of recent technology in providing innovative, efficient classroom instruction. Teachers will be "encouraged" by their school system administrators to use new technological tools, such as the microcomputer, in diagnosing student needs, preparing instructional materials, and monitoring the progress of students. Are economic educators and other social studies professionals prepared to assist teachers in the effective use of these new technologies?

Additional efforts must be expended at the school-system level to convince administrators of the importance of economic education for their teachers if they are to develop students who are economically literate. Industry has long recognized the importance of financial support for the continual development of its professionals and of research expenditures for the creation of new products. Are not the teachers of the nation's youth important enough to justify financial support when they undertake to update their knowledge base and refine their teaching skills? Are not the new creations of the next generation coming from our schools worth increased research expenditures in economic education?

It is hoped that the reader will not conclude this chapter with a pessimistic view of the present status of economic education for teachers. Innovative, successful programs are being conducted throughout the country. Many exciting, new programs are just being initiated by colleges and school systems. For educators interested in becoming involved in the economic education of teachers, the opportunities are challenging and many. The future is, indeed, bright. Why not make a commitment, however large or small, to become involved in that future?

BIBLIOGRAPHY

Agency for Instructional Television, *Trade-offs.* Bloomington, Indiana, 1978.

Clayton, G., "Trading-off for Trade-offs." Unpublished Manuscript. Normal: Illinois State U.: Depository for Economic Education Awards, 1979.

California State Board of Education, *College Preparation for Teaching Economics.* New York: Joint Council on Economic Education, 1969.

Davison, Donald G., *Master Curriculum Guide in Economics for the Nation's Schools: Part II, Strategies for Teaching Economics: Primary Level (Grades 1-3).* New York: Joint Council on Economic Education, 1977.

Frye, C., "An Examination of Statewide Mandates in Economic Education and the Programs Developed to Implement These Mandates." Master's Thesis, University of Central Florida at Orlando, 1979.

Highsmith, R., "A Study to Measure the Impact of In-Service Institutes on the Students of Teachers Who Have Participated," *Journal of Economic Education,* 5:2, Spring 1974, pp. 77-81.

Kourilsky, M., *Beyond Simulation: The Mini-Society Approach to Instruction in Economics and Other Social Sciences.* Los Angeles: Educational Resource Associates, Inc., 1974.

Moore, J.R. and P.L. Williams, "Trends in Social Studies Curricula and Graduation Competencies," *Theory and Research in Social Education,* Summer 1980, pp. 27-36.

Pipho, C., "Minimum Competency Testing in 1978: A Look at State Standards," *Phi Delta Kappan,* May, 1978, pp. 585-588.

Schneider, D.O. and R.L. VanSickle, "The Status of the Social Studies: The Publishers' Perspective," *Social Education,* October, 1979, pp. 461-465.

Townshend-Zellner, N., "How to Organize Economics Instruction for Teachers in In-Service Training Workshops." Mimeographed. Economic Literacy Project of the California State Universities and Colleges, 1977.

Wakin, E., "Raising the National EQ," *American Way,* July, 1980, pp. 24-27.

Weidenaar, D., "An Evaluation of the Economics Education Institute for College and University Social Studies Educators, 1976-77." Mimeographed. West Lafayette, Indiana: Purdue Center for Economic Education, 1977.

_____. *Master Curriculum Guide in Economics for the Nation's Schools: Part II, Strategies for Teaching Economics: Social Studies Methods.* New York: Joint Council on Economic Education (forthcoming).

Economic education is essential to a reasonable public grasp of the day-to-day operations of our system, just as better understanding by many business leaders concerning society's expectations of them is essential for a working partnership. Only economic education and business words and deeds together can hope to provide the legitimacy so essential to business firms if they are to play their role effectively at the center of a market-directed economy. To expect universal admiration to replace the present ambivalence in the American people's love-hate relationship with big business is to be naive indeed. Economic education can surely help greatly—but it is only a necessary, not a sufficient, condition.

G. L. Bach
Frank E. Buck Professor of Economics and Public Policy,
Stanford University

The tragedy of social science, particularly of economic education, is that we separate true and false from good and evil. This surgery undermines not only the principles of religious leaders, but also the value system of Adam Smith. Smith divided his lectures in Glasgow into four parts: natural theology, ethics, justice, and expediency (wealth and power). . . . if you want our youth to invent a better future than the present trends indicate, you have to introduce Adam Smith not only as a scientist, but also as a professor of moral philosophy.

Lawrence Senesh
Professor of Economics
University of Colorado

Courtesy of University of West Florida Information Services

CHAPTER 7

Ideology and Economic Education

JACK L. NELSON AND KENNETH CARLSON

Of the three key words in the title of this chapter, one—"ideology"—is commonly perceived as ambiguous, heavily loaded with values, and strongly partisan, often with negative overtones. "Economic" and "education" are typically used in conversations, newspapers, and classrooms as though they were neutral or positive terms which have clear and well-understood meanings. Ideology, then, as it is commonly used, might appear to be antithetical to economic education. Yet, any attempt at separation of ideology from economic education is fraudulent. Economics, far from being pure truth, involves ideologies, some of which are contradictory and competing. Furthermore the form and nature of education are ideological at their base. Ideology, economics, and education are intertwined concepts.

This intertwining of ideology, economics, and education is evident in several aspects of economic education. Schools exist in social, political, and economic settings that exert influence over what is taught to youth. Special-interest groups pressure school boards, publishers, administrators, and news media to control the content of economics teaching. Teacher education depends upon college and university programs and the kind of exposure to economics given to pre-service and in-service teachers. Teaching materials and practices reflect the dominant views of economics expected in textbooks, films, and other resources. Publishers exist in the economic system and will avoid controversy which may affect their market; special-interest groups with particular economic views produce teaching material and provide it free for classroom use; and many teachers are cautious about economic topics that are controversial, because the ideas are outside the mainstream of politically acceptable viewpoints or because they feel inadequately prepared. Each of these (political environment, teacher education, and teaching materials and practice) is a point where ideology, economics, and education intertwine.

One current example of ideology and economic education is the provision by major American businesses of endowed "free enterprise" chairs for professors who are to teach a particular form of economics. Fred Hechinger, writing in *Saturday Review*, made the following comments on this approach to economics instruction in colleges and universities where teachers and other professionals are prepared:

83

Some of the big companies make no bones about the one-sided aims of the programs that they bankroll. The Goodyear Tire and Rubber Company, for instance, has given Kent State University $250,000 to set up the Goodyear Professorship of Free Enterprise. The retired advertising executive who holds the new post says frankly that he regards it as a golden opportunity to act as a "business missionary." A businessman who endowed Ohio State with a similar chair has said, "Since universities teach youngsters about the Communist, socialist and fascist systems, [I feel] there is a real need to teach about American free enterprise." (Hechinger, 1978, p. 14)

Hechinger notes that the assumption that colleges are not already teaching basic facts about free enterprise, market economy, and competition is "patently absurd." And he points out that the endowment of professorships obligated to free enterprise is incompatible with the presumed tradition of autonomy in universities and the tenets of academic freedom.

On the other hand, William Simon, former U.S. Treasury Secretary, has written to complain that "most private funds, inevitably from business itself, flow ceaselessly to the very institutions which are philosophically committed to the destruction of capitalism" (Simon, 1978, p. 228). Simon notes the angry resignation of Henry Ford II from the Ford Foundation because of the Foundation's alleged antipathy to capitalism. To redress this bias in the economic ideology of the intellectual community, Simon urges "genuinely principled businessmen" to fund a "powerful counterintelligentsia" (Simon, pp. 223, 229). He also says that "business must cease the mindless subsidizing of colleges and universities whose departments of economics, government, politics and history are hostile to capitalism and whose faculties will not hire scholars whose views are otherwise" (Simon, p. 231).

Teaching materials prepared by corporations for school use also show the influence of ideology on economics education. Sheila Harty's recent book examines this activity and indicates her point of view in the title, *Hucksters in the Classroom* (Harty, 1980). The book discusses illustrations of economic bias and propaganda produced by various industries and made easily available for school use. Many teachers, often inadequately prepared in economics, find these handy and attractive materials very useful in classrooms and do not examine them critically.

Labor unions have also produced ideological teaching materials for economics classes, and, although they are not as easily available as business-oriented material, they too are often presented uncritically to students. Labor unions are quite sensitive to their disadvantage in the competition for the minds of youth. As early as 1923, the AFL sponsored a study of the school textbook treatment of labor unions (Berelson, 1952). Academic studies since then have repeatedly confirmed the diagnosis that labor unions do not fare well in textbooks and other teaching materials (Anyon, 1979; Doherty, 1964; Linton, 1965; Scoggins, 1966).

Despite its current scientific and technical image, economics remains a subject heavily entwined with politics and morality. As Kenneth Boulding (1964, 1968) pointed out, economics remains a "moral science," whose central problem is that of value, and "value is but a step from virtue." It is impossible to avoid questions of value and, thus, ideology in economics, even where the focus of the study is on technical terminology and econometric formulae. Economists do look at the trade-offs among conflicting economic goals. Furthermore, definitions of terms like "scarcity," "labor," "profit," and "efficiency" depend upon ideological perspectives. Economic statistics are often used to support interpretations based upon values.

Making judgments about the role that ideology should play in economic education depends upon which definition of ideology is applied. Ideological views shape the social and political setting of schools, the economic education of teachers, and the materials which teachers use to convey economic information to students. This chapter presents a definition of ideology, a brief examination of some aspects of teaching economics, a proposal for an economic education rationale, and suggestions for teachers who face problems in this area.

DEFINITIONS AND DIMENSIONS OF IDEOLOGY

Definitions of ideology begin with the coinage of the term by Destutt de Tracy (1754–1836), a French philosopher who used it to refer to the rigorous empirical analysis of the human mind. The most neutral or positive definition of ideology is contained in *Webster's New World Dictionary:* "the study of ideas, their nature and source." Just as biology, psychology, and other "ologies" are the studies of aspects of human knowledge, ideology as the study of ideas would be a well-suited—perhaps the most significant—subject for teaching in schools.

Ideology, however, has become freighted with values, as the following suggests:

According to Engels, ideology is a process accomplished by the so-called thinker consciously, no doubt, but with a false consciousness. (Jakubowski, 1936, 1976, p. 98)

Leaders of the French Revolution adopted the term ideology and it took on political overtones associated with republicanism and radical ideas hostile to Napoleon. (Aiken, 1957, p. 16)

Mannheim . . . labeled as "ideology" the conservative, interest-based and biased ideas of the dominant class in society. (Christenson et al., 1971, p. 4)

What Marx and Engels . . . call "ideology" includes not only the theory of knowledge and politics, but also metaphysics, ethics, religion, and indeed any "form of consciousness" which expresses the basic attitudes or commitments of a social class. (Aiken, 1957, p. 17)

Ideology is the conversion of ideas into social levers . . . for the ideologue, truth arises in action . . . . (Bell, 1967, pp. 370-371)

In this chapter, ideology shall be used to incorporate the following dimensions, a variation of those used by Lane (1962, pp. 13–16) in his discussion of political ideology:

1. moral, ethical, and normative views of major human endeavors, including economic and educational relationships. (Examples: those who invest the most deserve the highest rewards; those whose needs are greatest deserve the greatest support.)

2. a rationalization of group interests. (Examples: the upper classes, having higher intelligence, are more suited to leadership; the upper classes, by simple accident of birth, have oppressed and exploited workers throughout history.)

3. an essential position or argument from which significant attitudes and actions are derived. (Examples: schools should develop good work habits and job skills in students of lower ability; all students deserve equal access to education and to economic resources.)

4. implied theories of human nature and cause-and-effect. (Examples: humans are naturally competitive, so free enterprise causes higher productivity; humans are basically cooperative, so communism provides less alienation.)

The Interdependency

Using these dimensions of ideology, it is easy to see how economics and education are intertwined with ideology. Social studies teachers are constantly faced with economics-related questions like:

* Who gets what and how much?
* What justifies individual, class, or national inequalities in wealth and access?
* What is the nature of profit?
* What is the cause of poverty?
* What is classified as work?
* What is the nature of a market?
* What is the proper role of government in economics?
* What should be produced and how should it be allocated?
* Should capitalism or socialism provide the basis for a global economic system?
* What are the bases for determining the true costs of products?
* Who should control resources, production, land, labor, capital?

And educational questions like:

* Who should be educated? For what purposes?
* Who should pay the costs of education?
* Is education like a business with emphasis on efficiency?
* Who should have access to the "best" education?
* How do liberal studies differ from vocational?
* What curriculum is suited to what students?
* What subjects are of most importance?
* Who gets what treatment in schools?
* On what basis does the school separate students?
* What is the relation between socio-economic class and schooling?
* Who controls the schools? Who should?

Such questions can only be dealt with by reference to ideology. Economic justifications and relationships are subject to ideological influence. Rationales for schooling and for differentiating among students are also subject to ideology. And the ideologies which people acquire, and on which they make major decisions, are subject to economic conditions and to the kind of education they have received.

The teaching of economics, then, involves ideological considerations from economics and education. In economic education the choice of basic economic framework, the teaching materials, the economic views learned and taught by the teacher, the school environment, the community and social context within which the school exists, and social traditions and mores convey ideological perspectives to students. Often these perspectives go unexamined in schools and society. The ideology is taught and learned as truth, rather than as ideas which are subject to challenge. Some of the ideology is consciously selected, such as teaching students to be "wise consumers," but much of it is very subtle and pervasive. Teaching for wise consumption, for example, does not usually raise deeper questions about the nature of a consumer society or provide a critical assessment of larger economic relationships into which consumers fit. Consumer economics is often justified on the basis of its necessity in contemporary society without concern for a critical evaluation of that society. Students may be taught how to compute loan charges, but not how to analyze the social and economic impact of usury laws and discriminatory banking practices in order to make changes according to their assessment.

The Political Setting of Economic Education

In our form of democratic government, elected representatives determine public policy, and that policy reflects some perception of popular sentiment. Presumably, authority ultimately resides in the people, even the authority to act foolishly or shortsightedly. This is the overriding principle of democracy.

In education, the fit between popular belief and official policy is likely to be closer than in any other area of government. Local control of the schools, often entailing school-board elections and school budget votes, gives the public direct and almost immediate command of policy. An outpouring of indignant citizens at a school-board meeting can effect a policy or a policy change that same evening.

The active authority of the people over their schools has meant the inculcation of popular prejudices. Two redeeming features of this are (1) that the prejudices are at least of a tacitly majoritarian nature, and (2) that the localization of schools means a localization and, to some extent, a diversity of prejudices. One of the most common subject areas for the indoctrination of popular prejudices is economics, but here the diversity of the prejudices is along a fairly constricted continuum.

Ideology in American Economic Education

Economic ideologies introduced in American schools run the narrow gamut from liberalism to conservatism—i.e., from slightly left of center to slightly right of center. Anything further out is usually not taught or taught about; it is taught against. Obviously, there are exceptions to this—radicalized teachers of the sixties who preached various forms of socialism are an illustration.

In addition to the inculcation of liberal-conservative ideologies, there is another kind of economic instruction which is quite common. It is what we shall call "technical" economics, where terminology and formulae are taught and substantive values are avoided except as they are discussed in evaluating policy goals. Such instruction gives pupils a vocabulary useful for understanding concepts and topics common to all economic systems. It has scientific orientation. It cannot easily be accused of being a support of the power structure (or a subversion of it), although it does convey values by not expressing or challenging its own assumptions.

The cautiousness of both liberal-conservative and technical economics instruction among social studies teachers is not without warrant. More extreme economic ideologies have had historical enactments of terrifying proportions. On the right, there was the national socialism of the Third Reich, with its barbaric genocide and ruthless expansionism. On the left, there has been the communism of Soviet Russia, with its massive purges and its Gulag subcivilization.

The hegemony of liberal-conservative and technical economic instruction among economic educators can also be explained in terms of the widespread conviction that anything beyond the norm is hopelessly unadaptable to the American scene, or that it is necessarily un-American. Americans are thought to have forged an eclectic economic system out of long experience with economic experimentation. That system is an amalgam of left and right elements held in precarious balance and constantly fine-tuned with further tinkering. America was originally a fertile soil for radicalism, and some believe that it remains so (Revel, 1972), but there is little evidence of it in schooling.

In summary, there are three themes evident in American economic education. First, economic education is a democratically determined enterprise depending upon local control. Second, this enterprise is characterized by caution and the inculcation of a narrow spectrum of ideologies. Third, the nature of economic education in American public schools is understandable on a number of historical grounds.

The caution exhibited in economic education in the United States draws from the political setting and affects teacher education, teacher practices, and teaching materials. Interviews with individuals who have been involved with economic education in America illustrate its ideological—and cautious—context.

Comments on Ideology and Economic Education in the United States

Suzanne Helburn, Professor of Economics at the University of Colorado-Denver, and director of major economic education projects in the 1960s, made the following comments during an interview:

[Several states] have passed mandated courses or units in "Free Enterprise Economics." The very use of the term "free enterprise," which is not a scientific term but is an ideological one, gives some idea of the intent of legislatures.

Even though there is an attempt at objectivity [among economists], our basic way of evaluating the performance of an economic system tends to be efficiency. From our perspective, the socialist countries are not as efficient; there is wastage. From a socialist viewpoint, the market economy wastes resources on advertising, product differentiation, and consumerism. But I have never seen that argument in a high school text. At the university level, we have our own bias about the superiority of the market mechanism as an allocative mechanism and as a motivational system for people, and we tend to judge the socialist countries by those criteria. We don't use social justice or balanced economic development as criteria, and these are areas where the socialist countries could come off better than we do.

When we started developing our materials for Economics in Society (1963), we examined available materials for teaching economics. I was appalled at that time at the bias in materials. These were from the National Association of Manufacturers and the AFL-CIO, among others. The materials gave a very simple-minded economics. That kind of [sponsored] material has proliferated since that time.

A teacher should be as truthful as possible with students. A mature person with a value system is a good model for students, but a teacher should use those values as a way to get students exploring ideas. Ideology up front should help make teaching exciting. Ideology shouldn't be imposed, but should be expressed and examined. Students should look at [economic] questions from different points of view. (Helburn, 1980)

Howard Schober, Executive Director of the Louisiana State Council on Economics Education, and a recent secondary classroom teacher of economics, remarked:

Economic education in the United States is definitely pro-capitalist and pro-corporation. Those views are found in virtually all materials. It has to be because of the funding base for economic education. . . . This predisposes people in economic education to orient materials and teacher education toward capitalism and corporate views. You don't find advocacy for socialism — or even for labor's views much. The Joint Council on Economic Education and its various centers offer some opportunity for broader and more objective treatment because of their affiliation with universities and colleges. (Schober, 1980)

Marilyn Kourilsky, Director of the Center for Economics Education at UCLA and an economic educator who has conducted teacher workshops in 37 states, commented:

The role of economic education should be exposition as opposed to imposition. Many of the organizations devoted to economic education are advocates of a particular philosophy as opposed to being conveyors of information or inquirers. They are often agents of indoctrination rather than inquiry. (Kourilsky, 1980)

Comments on Ideology and Economic Education in Western Europe

Similar considerations of political setting, teacher education, and materials influence economic teaching in other countries. West Germany and England are lands politically and economically associated with the United States, and which exhibit some of the same ideological caution as occurs here, but they appear to have somewhat more latitude in teacher practice and course content.

Georg Groth, Professor of Theory of Economics and Labor and Professor of

Education at the University of Berlin, made the following comments during an interview about economic education in West Germany:

All teachers of social studies feel restricted in some way. You can teach about communism, but you can't be a communist. In the schools, talking about socialism is very acceptable, but a teacher who talks about communism may get in trouble. Our leading political party, the Social Democrats, refer to socialism as one part of their program, so it is acceptable in schools. A teacher can discuss the problem of communism—historically—but not as a probability nowadays [for West Germany]. Teachers with Marxist views will have trouble with the parents and maybe with school officials. There is pressure from the government and from parents.

We have a lot of professors in universities who are Marxists and their students can get degrees, but there are problems for them [the students] to get a job in teaching.

Teaching materials are reviewed by a board which has trade union and employer representatives as well as classroom teachers and professors. If materials come from a company and are too narrow, they will be rejected; if board-recommended materials are too controversial, the government will not accept them and they won't be purchased for school use. (Groth, 1980)

Geoff Whitty, Lecturer in Education at the University of Bath, England, and a consulting editor of *Theory and Research in Social Education,* responded to interview questions on economic education in England with the following:

Most economics teaching [in Britain] is dominated by a perspective which sees pure, free market as the ideal. There is a duality between this ideal and what actually goes on. The bias in schools is that the pure market ought to work and it doesn't work—that's seen as an anomaly rather than something that requires a different theory or perspective. What is excluded from most economics teaching is the examination of alternative perspectives on the concept of market which might better explain what is really happening. Most economics teachers have degrees in economics and teach only students going on to universities. These teachers are the product of university departments of economics. They may not consciously exclude different economics perspectives; they simply don't consider them. The exclusion of Marxist perspectives, for instance, is a feature of most academic economics departments in universities. . . . Economics is not taught much to the masses of students who do not take the examinations. (Whitty, 1980)

Barry DuFour, Lecturer in Social Science Education at the University of Leicester, England, and author of books on social education, confirmed Professor Whitty's views and added general comments as follows:

Economics tends to be treated in a very narrow, pseudo-scientific manner—for example, whole questions of trade unions and industrial relations are often dealt with as technical problems rather than as social or political problems. A strike of underground [subway] workers in London would not be examined in terms of class struggle or political conflict, but as a technical economic question (salaries, work hours, employment conditions, etc.).

Even though there is a very respectable new brand of Marxist economics in the U.K., it is very much squeezed out. I know of only one professor in Britain who would call himself Marxist. There may be others, but it is not popular.

I think the ideology in economics is fairly narrow. Students of economics are often not introduced to a whole range of perspectives and controversies in economics. Economics, out of all the social subjects, is one of the key areas crying out for critical analysis. (DuFour, 1980)

P.L. Waller, Adviser for Business Studies and Economics at the Teachers' Centre, London Borough of Waltham Forest, believes that teachers in England have considerable freedom and tend to be objective in economic instruction. He notes the close tie of the course syllabus in economics to the examination system and the high proportion of the syllabus devoted to descriptive information rather than analysis. The syllabi say very little about opposing or divergent viewpoints, although Waller indicates that divergent views are permitted (Waller, 1980).

David Whitehead, Head of the Department of Economics and Business Studies at the University of London Institute of Education, states that the economics syllabus deals principally with markets and how the system works, rather than a critical analysis of the system and its underlying values. Although teachers can submit a proposed syllabus to the examining board, according to Whitehead, value-loaded ones are likely to be thrown out. The teaching and examining system does not encourage divergent views (Whitehead, 1980).

A Rationale for Expanding Economic Education in America

The ideological basis for economics instruction in the United States may be similar to that in West Germany and England, according to the above observations, but that does not mean the status quo should be accepted uncritically. Discontent with the narrow ideological spectrum represented in economic teaching suggests a need to reformulate a rationale for economic education which takes more extreme ideologies into account. New ideas to challenge current orthodoxies can lead to improved economics instruction, especially at the high school and college level. In recent decades, the natural sciences have become highly self-critical, and much attention is given to the scrutiny of assumptions which had previously been taken for granted. The social sciences, especially one as susceptible to ideological influence as economics, should do no less.

Several states have gone so far as to mandate that teaching about communism must be only to show it as evil (Nelson, 1976). These mandates make explicit two assumptions; namely, that capitalism is the necessary economic system for democracy, while Marxism or socialism necessarily precludes democracy. Democratic socialism is dismissed as a contradiction in terms that can be taken seriously only by naive people like Michael Harrington and Irving Howe (Harrington, 1973; Howe, 1980). The censorious approach to radical economic ideologies may well defeat its own purpose. Rather than safeguarding young people from pernicious error, it may give this "error" the allure of forbidden fruit.

David Riesman (1956) and Jules Henry (1965) have each contended that social studies education is an exercise of such timidity that its major yield is stupidity. Economic education has hardly been an exception to this harsh indictment of social studies in general (although it has escaped the utter mindlessness of "one damn thing after another" history). In some classrooms there has been a concentration on the memorization and regurgitation of facts and jargon. Such instruction results in a tyranny of terminology in which the labeling of phenomena is thought to be tantamount to the explanation of the phenomena. In the case of liberal-conservative economic instruction, students are often treated as passive recipients of someone else's received truth. Teaching about divergent economic views (both from the right and left) should involve an attempt at factual accuracy as well as the open inquiry by students which may lead to conclusions that are not predetermined by the teacher or social convention. It should not involve the inculcation of beliefs for or against these divergent views.

It is axiomatic that people think about that which concerns them, and that thinking is an internal struggle to understand and cope. Understanding requires alternative explanations, and coping demands alternative solutions. Perfect understanding of complex economic conditions has not been achieved by economists, and the person with a simplistic orthodoxy is worse than wrong—he is resistant to doubt. Providing simple answers to students does not develop in them a tolerance for ambiguity, and ambiguity is a reigning reality in the economic realm. What students need most of all is an exposure to a variety of ideologies and the ability to use basic economic concepts to analyze the empirical and logical bases of the ideologies. A course with these objectives will not leave students with an uncritical understanding, but with an appreciation for the difficulty of acquiring understanding.

Economic Socialization and Economic Education

Among the positive reasons for a new rationale for economic education is to fulfill the obligations of education. A major purpose for teaching economics is to provide economic literacy, which implies something more than the memorization and regurgitation of economic information. In language, one who is adequately literate obviously has more than a bare grasp of elementary reading, pronunciation, and writing skills. Literacy in contemporary society includes the development of a level of sophistication in language skills, thoughtful consideration, and critical judgment. Similarly, economic literacy incorporates some sophistication in the understanding of economic concepts, thoughtful consideration of those concepts and their application, and critical judgment of the concepts and their consequences for society and individuals.

Economic literacy in these terms is more than the standard expectation of economic socialization, which is that children will uncritically assimilate the economic dogma and ideology of their environment. The school's role in this narrow view of economic socialization is to provide only socially approved ideas about economic questions and to train the child to accept this ideology. Wherever a student attends school, in the U.S., the U.S.S.R., China, South Africa, Brazil, or any other country, that student is taught the prevailing national economic view as truth and that a divergent view is either nonexistent or blatantly false. Out-of-school socialization from family, the media, and peer groups tends to reinforce the prevailing economic ideology. And the hidden curriculum of the school, through social-class patterns of student interaction and segregation, strengthens this belief (Carlton, 1977, Giroux and Penna, 1979).

This essentially conservative function of socialization is lifelong and common to all societies. It explains a general reluctance to change and the deep-set ideological commitments of different societies to their own views.

There is another aspect of socialization, however, which assumes that change is a basic condition of all societies, and that people need to understand divergent views in order to make better decisions about their own futures. Enlightened democracy and a rational global society depend on it. This form of socialization inculcates a thinking process that encourages open inquiry and rational decision-making about topics that are controversial. At its best, this kind of socialization is the heart of education. It is not mechanical and does not profess to give truth; it is liberating, thoughtful, and truth-seeking. Education is based on the study of ideas—competing, complementary, and controversial. Economic ideas are certainly worthy of such treatment. Economic literacy raised to the level of critical examination of controversial topics is what economic education should provide.

As support for this notion of education, we cite the report of the Rockefeller Foundation Commission on the Humanities (Lyman, 1980). The commission consisted of 32 eminent scholars, including the presidents of Yale, Smith, University of Chicago, and Tulane; and it came to the conclusion that the recent emphasis on basic skills has undermined the task of teaching students how to think. The report calls for critical thinking to be included among the "basic skills" and to be so treated by the U.S. Department of Education.

Suggestions for Teachers

Classroom teachers and others involved in the process of schooling need to examine continually the ideological dimensions of their work. This is especially true in areas of curriculum like economics which are subject to controversy. Furthermore, the best defense for academic freedom in social studies instruction is teacher competence in handling divergent views in the classroom. To become more competent, teachers must:

• Become increasingly knowledgeable about changing patterns in global, national, and regional politics, and their effects on economics.

• Understand the local community: its social and political structure and the vocal and/or thoughtful critics.

• Become familiar with state and local laws, regulations, and unwritten expectations about economic teaching.

• Become knowledgeable about constitutional and academic freedom policies and practices, and about agencies to contact for assistance when teacher and student freedoms are threatened. (For example, American Civil Liberties Union; the National Council for the Social Studies; local district policies and teacher contracts; special issue of *Social Education*, April, 1975.)

• Develop and maintain open communication with administrators, colleagues, and parents in regard to the educational rationale and classroom practices utilized. There is often more support for good professional teaching of controversy than teachers recognize.

• Become familiar with techniques for dealing with controversy in the classroom and the community. (For example, Foshay, 1974; Nelson and Michaelis, 1980, Chapter 8).

- Develop competence in economics, both mainstream and divergent views, through such avenues as: reading, course work, institutes, conferences, discussion, and debate.
- Develop a critical skepticism about the ideological framework of readings, courses, and related experiences.
- Seek school district in-service workshops that include exploration of divergent economic views, and methods of incorporating them into curriculum and instruction.
- Participate in professional activities through such agencies as NCSS and the Joint Council on Economic Education; promote more concern with ideological interests and divergent views in these organizations.
- Provide a classroom environment which encourages rational inquiry into economic controversy and which stimulates critical insights on the part of students.
- Bring in materials from differing ideologies and perspectives for classroom analysis.
- Prepare students to be competent and skeptical consumers of economic information, ideologies, and propaganda.
- Invite local representatives of divergent views to participate in class discussions.
- Refrain from indoctrination of economic ideologies; be an active classroom participant and leader, but provide for critical examination of all views, including the teacher's.
- Examine materials for ideological view; encourage student examination on similar grounds.
- Develop a critical skepticism about sponsored materials — those free materials provided by business, labor, or other groups.
- Assist students in preparing a set of guidelines and criteria against which to judge sponsored materials, commercials, advertising, and standard school materials.
- Seek examples of ideological views in economics from as wide a spectrum as possible; keep these as a resource for classroom use.

SUMMARY AND CONCLUSION

This chapter suggests that ideology, economics, and education are intertwined concepts. Ideology is identified as a set of beliefs which convey moral views, group interests, implied theories about human behavior, and standards for judging people. The ideology of economics taught in schools in the United States is narrow and restrictive, based primarily on limited concepts of capitalism. The social/political setting of schools, the nature of teacher education, and typical teacher practices and teaching materials reinforce the narrow economic ideology taught. As a result, education in economics for an enlightened democracy suffers.

A rationale is proposed for expanding economic education in the United States by using the existence of divergent ideologies to develop critical skepticism about economic ideas. A number of suggestions are presented for teachers who desire to pursue this expanded economic education.

Ideology in economic education is not necessarily unfortunate. All economic views convey some ideological interests. Education in economics becomes dysfunctional when a particular economic ideology is indoctrinated rather than critically examined. Without the needed skills and opportunities to examine divergent views and explore ideologies, students are not adequately educated to participate fully in an enlightened democracy.

REFERENCES

Aiken, Henry D., *The Age of Ideology*. New York: G. Braziller, 1957.

American Civil Liberties Union, *Academic Freedom in the Secondary School*. New York: ACLU, 1971.

Anyon, Jean, "Elementary Social Studies Textbooks and Legitimating Knowledge," *Theory and Research in Social Education*, 6:3, 40-55, 1978.

Bell, Daniel, *The End of Ideology: The Exhaustion of Political Ideals in the 50s*. Glencoe, Illinois: Free Press, 1967.

Berelson, Bernard, *Content Analysis in Communication Research*. Glencoe, Illinois: The Free Press, 1952.

Bork, Robert H., "Who Will Speak for Capitalism?" *Reason*, July, 1979, pp. 29-31.

Boulding, Kenneth, *Beyond Economics*. Ann Arbor: University of Michigan Press, 1968; including the essay, "Is Economics Necessary?" from *The Scientific Monthly*, 68, 4 (April, 1949).

Buckley, William, *God and Man at Yale*. Chicago: Henry Regnery Co., 1951.

Carlton, Eric, *Ideology and Social Order*. London: Routledge and Kegan Paul, 1977.

Christenson, Reo, et al., *Ideologies and Modern Politics*. Dodd, Mead and Co., 1971.

Davidson, Paul, "Post-Keynesian Economics: Solving the Crisis in Economic Theory," *The Public Interest*, Special Edition, 1980.

Doherty, Robert, *Teaching Industrial Relations in High Schools: A Survey*. Ithaca: New York State School of Industrial and Labor Relations, 1964.

DuFour, Barry, Interview, Guildford, England, July, 1980.

Feuer, Lewis, *Ideology and the Ideologists*. New York: Oxford Press, 1975.

Field, William, "The Conceits of the Keynesians," *Reason*, November, 1979, pp. 33ff.

Foshay, Arthur W., *Coping with Community Controversy*. Boulder, Colorado: Social Science Education Consortium Publication #173, 1974.

Giroux, Henry and Anthony Penna, "Social Education in the Classroom: The Dynamics of the Hidden Curriculum," *Theory and Research in Social Education*, 7:1, 21-42, Spring, 1979.

Gonzalez, Gilbert, "Education and Monopoly Capitalism," *The Insurgent Sociologist*, Fall, 1977, pp. 25-41.

Groth, Georg, Interview, Guildford, England, July, 1980.

Harrington, Michael, *Socialism*. New York: Bantam, 1972.

Harty, Sheila, *Hucksters in the Classroom.* Washington, D. C.: Center for Responsive Legislation, 1980.

Hayek, Friedrich, *The Road to Serfdom.* University of Chicago, 1944.

Hechinger, Fred, "The Corporation in the Classroom," *Saturday Review*, Sept. 16, 1978, pp. 14, 15.

Heilbroner, Robert, *Marxism: For and Against.* New York: W.W. Norton, 1979.

Helburn, Suzanne, Interview, Guildford, England, July, 1980.

Henry, Jules, *Culture Against Man.* New York: Vintage, 1965.

Howe, Irving (ed.), *Dissent* (any of the issues of this journal).

Hunt, Maurice and Lawrence Metcalf, *Teaching High School Social Studies.* New York: Harper and Row, 1956.

Inglis, Fred, *Ideology and the Imagination.* London: Cambridge University Press, 1975.

Jakubowski, Franz, *Ideology and Superstructure in Historical Materialism* (1936), trans. by Anne Booth. New York: St. Martin's Press, 1976.

Kourilsky, Marilyn, Telephone interview, September, 1980.

Lane, Robert E., *Political Ideology.* New York: The Free Press of Glencoe, 1962.

Laslett, John and Seymour Lipset, *Failure of a Dream?* Garden City, New York: Anchor Books, 1974.

Linton, Thomas, *An Historical Examination of the Purposes and Practices of the United Automobile Workers.* University of Michigan Press, 1965.

Lyman, Richard et al., *The Humanities in American Life.* University of California Press, 1980.

Mermelstein, David (ed.), *Economics: Mainstream Readings and Radical Critiques.* New York: Random House, 1970.

Nelson, Jack L. and John U. Michaelis, *Secondary Social Studies: Instruction, Curriculum, Evaluation.* Englewood Cliffs, New Jersey: Prentice-Hall, 1980.

Nelson, Jack L., "Nationalistic vs. Global Education: An Examination of National Bias in the Schools and Its Implications for a Global Society," *Theory and Research in Social Education*, August, 1976, pp. 33-50.

Revel, Jean-Francois, *Without Marx or Jesus.* New York: Doubleday, 1972.

Riesman, David, *Constraint and Variety in American Education.* Lincoln: University of Nebraska, 1956.

Scoggins, Will, *Labor in Learning.* Los Angeles: UCLA Center for Labor Research and Education, 1966.

Simon, William, *A Time for Truth.* New York: McGraw-Hill, 1978.

Social Education, Special issue on academic freedom, edited by Todd Clark, April, 1975.

Theobald, Robert, *The Economics of Abundance.* New York: Pitman, 1970.

Waller, Peter L., Personal Correspondence, September, 1980.

Whitehead, David, Personal Correspondence, August, 1980.

Whitty, Geoff, Interview, Guildford, England, July, 1980. Personal correspondence, November, 1980.

Courtesy of J. Pennington, Louisiana Council on Economic Education

The economic teaching of the late eighteenth, nineteenth, and the early twentieth centuries was of the sort that viewed men and women as victims of impersonal, economic, political, and social forces which were beyond their control. In contrast, the keynote of today's social science thinking is a belief in human capacity to identify and analyze the problems of living and working together, and a determination to do something toward ameliorating situations created by nature or by man's past bungling. Economic research and teaching have, during recent decades, been reoriented from a philosophy of resigned adaptation to one of positive policy making and social planning, both private and public.

Edwin G. Nourse,
First Chairperson of the
President's Council of Economic Advisers

CHAPTER 8

A Perspective for Meeting Our Persistent Economic Education Problems

GEORGE L. FERSH

Many years ago I had the good fortune to acquire an illuminating concept that has served to help me achieve perspective about the quest for knowledge and the solution of problems. The universal genius, Albert Einstein, avowed that as he grew older he was increasingly aware of the inadequacies of his knowledge. To explain why he believed this was so, he drew a small circle on the backboard, a larger circle, and then a still larger one. He stated that the increased size of each of the circles represented his growth in knowledge and experiences through the years. Running his finger around the circumference of the smallest circle, he pointed out that in his early years what he did not know was related to the realm of knowledge within the circle that he did know. Then, with gentle and genuine humility, he ran his finger around the next larger circle and the largest, and he let his lesson sink in. The succinct message was that we may expect that the more you know and do, the more will be your contact with what you realize you do not know and have not done. It is a message that puts into perspective the modesty and caution one generally encounters on the part of the well-informed, and the dogmatism and haste that one generally finds in the ill-informed.

I have chosen to begin this chapter by referring to Einstein's concept, so that its purpose and content will be viewed in a similar perspective. The presence of persistent problems in economic education is not a reflection that we have not grown in knowledge and experience about the field in the past thirty years. It is, rather, a reflection that because we now know so much more about economic education, we are capable of perceiving how much more there is to know and do. Our circle of knowledge and experience about economic education embraces not only potential opportunities and problems, but also includes an understanding of opportunities and problems which existed in the past but were unknown to us at that time.

A look back will help us to look ahead. About thirty years ago, a representative group of educators, economists, and economic practitioners were drawn together by their common interest in improving the teaching of economics in our nation's schools and colleges. Building upon a common concern, which they called economic illiteracy, the group established an organization, the Joint

Council on Economic Education (JCEE), based on broad principles of being nonprofit, nonpolitical, and nonpartisan. The aim of the JCEE, stated in general terms in its Certificate of Incorporation, was to engage in activities that would bring about a wider knowledge and understanding of the principles of economics and operation of our American economy. The organization focused on elementary and secondary schools and on teacher education institutions to guide them in making their full contribution to the furtherance of economic and social understanding. As general procedure, the Joint Council conducted its activities by developing cooperative working relationships with (and among) nonprofit educational organizations and other groups interested in economic education.

Those who launched the Joint Council were sufficiently seasoned by a wide range of experiences to identify major areas of policy and programs which would present them with immediate problems in the process of achieving their broad aims. Through research, discussion, and debate, they reached conclusions and took steps to deal with overt problems so that the organization and effort could get underway. From their experiences in the educational and economic worlds, the organizers anticipated that unforeseen problems would emerge as the JCEE dealt with realities related to the field of economic education. New problems would have to be dealt with by their successors in the field. The Joint Council's experience has been cited here because it has been recognized as a major force in providing leadership for the improvement and expansion of economic education throughout the nation. Familiarity with its development, activities, and problems has provided me with a perception for identifying persistent problems in economic education and has given me guidance in dealing with them.

It is logical to have problems in a field as complex, controversial, growing, and changing as economic education. It is proper for economic educators to be forthright in acknowledging the existence of the persistent problems they face so that efforts can be focused on dealing with them separately and collectively. To accept the fact that there are and always will be persistent problems does not disregard or demean the significant accomplishments of the past thirty years. Rather, it testifies to the realism and vitality of the economic education movement and provides an agenda for continuing to recognize and remove major blockages to the advancement of economic education. It enables us to move outward to yet another of Einstein's concentric rings, with the understanding that some fundamental problems will persist in economic education.

The preceding chapters have included the exposition of accomplishments and knowledge gained, as well as the recognition of problems and knowledge to be gained. In some cases, the fundamental problems are explicit, such as the uncertain status of economic education with regard to the place of ideology and the inadequate implementation of teacher education. In the chapters dealing with curriculum development and evaluation, knowledge is shown to be available but it is evident that there are still obstacles to the widespread application and expansion of such knowledge in our nation's schools. The chapter stressing the development of decision-making ability *through* the use of economic content illustrates by its premise and approach the persistent problem of determining the relative importance of aims for economic education. The chapter relating economic education with the community illustrates the way in which unforeseen problems may arise from shifts in purpose and method, as well as discussing the procedures for implementation.

Veterans, novices, and recruits in the fields of social studies education and economic education may find the present chapter of service to their needs and plans. From the perspective of thirty years of involvement in all aspects of the field, the author identifies major problem areas related to economic education and specifies questions and issues that social studies educators will encounter within those areas. The problem areas discussed are essentially those that were recognized thirty years ago and are likely to be the continuing source of problems in the future. Veterans can determine which aspects of the problem areas identified have been especially persistent, and all readers can evaluate those which represent problems pertinent to their current responsibilities and activities. While some of the choices posed may be judged by some as not being difficult choices or as being problems only in particular circumstances, it is believed that there is value in exposing all social studies educators to a full range of issues. Having done so, where consideration, discussion, and evidence reveal that issues raised do not pose insurmountable obstacles, there can be confidence to move ahead. But where serious problems are recognized to exist, strategies for dealing with them can be devised with full knowledge that ultimate solutions may never be found.

The remainder of this chapter is an application of the decision-making models discussed by H. Michael Hartoonian. The problems of economic education are put in perspective, so that we can deal with them. The problem areas are identified, the nature of the problems is defined, and alternatives for policy and action are suggested for analysis. Those reading the chapter are invited to review the analysis and are challenged to take the next steps: evaluate the probable consequences of alternative choices within each of the problem areas, reach conclusions consistent with their findings and values, and then take action.

PERSPECTIVE FOR RECOGNIZING
PERSISTENT PROBLEMS IN ECONOMIC EDUCATION

In the following pages, eight persistent problem areas relating to economic education are identified. Within each, there is a series of issue-oriented questions which indicate the potentials for problems to exist and/or develop. Efforts to answer these questions will shape present and future curriculum activity in the social studies. As was stated in the Introduction to this Bulletin, social studies and economic education specialists have a mutuality of interest in working together on the answers to these questions.

1. What are the purposes of economic education?

A comprehensive, clear response to this question involves considering, deciding, and dealing with such matters as the following:

- Relative emphasis on roles as consumer, producer, and citizen.
- Relative emphasis on knowledge, skills, and behavior.
- Relative emphasis on values—none, personal, social.
- Relative emphasis on immediate, short-range, and long-range objectives.
- Relative emphasis on education and indoctrination.
- Relative emphasis on tradition and innovation.
- Relative emphasis on retention of status quo and change.
- Relative emphasis on levels of economic understanding sought.
- Relative emphasis on local, regional, national, international interests.

Although consensus has been reached on general statements bearing on the purposes of economic education, there is evidence in the preceding chapters and elsewhere that reaching an accord on these relative emphases remains a persistent problem for social studies and economic educators. While it is valuable to call attention to the range of diverse purposes of economic education so that school systems are aware of potential contributions and choices, it is not enough simply to advise teachers about them. Social studies departments must constantly reexamine the objectives of economic education and, in the process, come to tentative agreements on what are feasible objectives. To aim at achieving all worthy objectives through a single course or a single curriculum is foolish, because there is limited time to do all of that adequately. Furthermore, if we leave the judgment exclusively to individual teachers, we are likely to get variation within school systems that makes comprehensive and sequential curriculum development impossible.

Of all the purposes of economic education, what shall we ask the teachers in our school district to focus upon? This is a persistent problem because such factors as the status of achievement, community response, changing needs, and limited resources require that this question be faced on a continuing basis. Periodical reexamination and recommitment to objectives will provide guidelines for what should be taught and a means of measuring effectiveness in achieving the accepted purposes of economic education.

2. What substance from economics and about the economy do we provide for economic education?

A comprehensive, clear response to this question involves considering, deciding, and dealing with such matters as these:

- Relative emphasis on principles, concepts, institutions, problems.
- Relative emphasis on past, present, and future economic problems.
- Relative emphasis on personal and societal economic matters.
- Relative emphasis on knowledge, understanding, application, and action.
- Relative emphasis on descriptive and analytical materials.
- Relative emphasis on varied frames of reference and viewpoints.
- Relative emphasis on available data and research sources.
- Relative emphasis on U.S. economy and the global economy.

Although a broad framework for the content of economic education has been developed over the years, achieving agreement on the emphases remains a persistent problem for social studies and economic educators. This problem area deals with decisions about what we believe students should know to be considered economically literate and what we believe would be most useful for them to know. It is obvious that students are limited by ability, background, and time to learn all the good things economic educators might consider to be requirements. Furthermore many students will make limited use of some knowledge even if they are able to learn it.

Through the Master Curriculum Guide Project, developed by highly qualified people under the aegis of the Joint Council on Economic Education, school districts and individual social studies teachers have a basic conceptual framework to examine. Curriculum decisions in the 1980s are likely to deviate from the framework recommendations. Deviations will be related to such matters as the capacities and aspirations of students, the values and capacities of teachers, results of teaching experiences, availability of resource people and materials, and changing perceptions of what is most needed. It is essential that an operational consensus be achieved about the substance of economic education within school districts in order to have a basis for guiding instruction and measuring effectiveness. However, it can be expected there will be a continuing need to examine the validity of the consensus in the light of outcomes achieved and changing needs.

3. Where do we provide economic education?

A comprehensive, clear response to this question involves considering, deciding, and dealing with such matters as these:

- Relative emphasis on various grade levels.
- Relative emphasis throughout various courses of curriculum.
- Relative emphasis within the social studies.
- Relative emphasis on developmental approach and focused grades.
- Relative emphasis on integration and separate courses.
- Relative emphasis on schools and colleges.
- Relative emphasis on schools and community.
- Relative emphasis within formal education and out-of-school sources.

Although general guidelines for economic instruction have been developed pertinent to grade placement, course objectives, and using the community as a classroom, deciding where and when to teach economics will remain a persistent problem for social studies and economic educators. Continuous research needs to be conducted on the relationship of economic instruction to the broad aspects of learning readiness and teaching procedures. Research results will influence the hard decisions of where it is best to provide economic education and what economics is appropriate to teach at various grade levels or in courses selected for emphasis. Fully developed K–12 economics programs which are measurably effective are not available as yet, nor are there research results of the comparative effectiveness of economic education provided by colleges, communities, and out-of-school sources. Yet, while decisions about where to provide economic education are difficult, they have to be made by local school systems, so that responsibility for instruction can be established, guidance and materials can be provided, and the results can be evaluated. Here, again, although some current research results are conclusive and persuasive, there will always be a need to consider where to introduce content. Even with more knowledge about factors related to scope and sequence, there will be unknowns to ponder.

4. How do we provide economic education?

A comprehensive, clear response to this question involves considering, deciding, and dealing with such matters as these:

- Relative emphasis on teacher competency and inclusion within curriculum.
- Relative emphasis on standardized texts and localized materials.
- Relative emphasis on various teaching styles and techniques.
- Relative emphasis on various tools for teaching.

Although many excellent materials have been developed related to techniques and instructional products for delivering economic education, making decisions concerning delivery will remain a persistent problem for social studies and economic educators. Limitations of time and money make it difficult for teachers to become aware of the range of choices. Differences in teachers' backgrounds and styles of teaching have a bearing on the selection of methodology and teaching tools. School districts vary in their financial capacity to provide the means for in-service training of teachers and for the purchase of equipment and materials. Even where financial factors are not paramount, there are dilemmas about which methods and materials make the most effective use of time and energy. The consequences of using various methods must also be considered in terms of how they affect this broad range of student competencies for learning and applying economics. Since this is an area of continuing change and constant assessment of relative returns, it must be dealt with as a persistent problem.

5. How do we motivate strategic people to contribute to the improvement of economic education?

A comprehensive, clear response to this question involves considering, deciding, and dealing with such matters as these:

- Relative emphasis on personal gratification and social responsibility.
- Relative emphasis on self-motivation by teachers, schools, state departments of education, and colleges, and certification requirements.
- Relative emphasis on influencing teachers and influencing administrators.
- Relative emphasis on influencing schools and influencing communities.
- Relative emphasis on influencing economists and influencing educators.
- Relative emphasis on making contribution as service or for professional advancement.
- Relative emphasis on benefits and costs in advancing economic education.

Although many dedicated people have made commitments to the economic education movement over the past thirty years, maintaining a high level of motivation among both new and veteran leaders will remain a persistent problem for social studies and economic educators. We shall always need to motivate and recruit or run the risk of failure. Effective curriculum change deals with general aspects of human relations and also with institutional aspects of the education profession. Decisions in this area involve knowing how to apply psychology as well as how to manipulate authority. The quality of the decisions made will be a major factor in determining what is accomplished quantitatively and qualitatively in economic education. Identification of strategic people who can contribute most to the improvement of economic education requires skill and perception. Since the individuals who are strategic people change over time, and what influences them may also change, this problem area requires constant attention.

6. How do we equip teachers to contribute toward economic education?

A comprehensive, clear response to this question involves considering, deciding, and dealing with such matters as these:

- Relative emphasis on pre-service and in-service economic education for teachers.
- Relative emphasis on courses, consultants, and workshops.
- Relative emphasis on economics and educational applications in programs for teachers.
- Relative emphasis on aid from peers and from outsiders.
- Relative emphasis on self-developed, selected, and imposed materials.
- Relative emphasis on teacher-training in classroms and through outside experiences.
- Relative emphasis on self-evaluation, supervision, and evaluation through standardized tests.

Although outstanding economics courses for teachers have been developed and research results have provided guidance on effective techniques for equipping teachers with the requisite skills to become economic educators, the job will never be finished. Costs of instruction, limited time, diverse priorities, and institutional inertia will conspire to make teacher education a persistent problem for social studies and economic educators. There may be near unanimity that teacher performance is the key ingredient influencing the effectiveness of economic education, but there is far less agreement on when, where, how, and by whom the teacher can be equipped to contribute significantly to economic education.

While new research may lead to narrowing the viable choices available to teacher educators, school districts will still have to make hard choices as they tailor their staff -development programs to the needs of and the resources made available by the community. Also, with the constant changes in the needs of teachers, it can be assumed that colleges and universities committed to teacher education will continuously make adjustments based on an increasing number of experiences.

7. How can we continue to improve economic education?

A comprehensive, clear response to this question involves considering, deciding, and dealing with such matters as these:

- Relative emphasis on research, development, and dissemination.
- Relative emphasis on localized evaluation and standardized evaluation.
- Relative emphasis on quality or quantity.
- Relative emphasis on individuality and sharing standardized models.
- Relative emphasis on limited aims and extended aims.
- Relative emphasis on established and innovative.
- Relative emphasis on students lagging behind and advanced students.
- Relative emphasis on organizational structures and personnel.
- Relative emphasis on teacher education and materials development.

Although progress has been made and viewpoints have been expressed related to setting priorities, social studies and economic educators have a continuing need to assess the consequences of alternative program emphases, and they will be required to take positions in dealing with allocating scarce resources. Since everything cannot be done at once, there is the persistent problem of deciding what is most important among all the important component parts of the economic education equation.

The decisions and tasks involved in improving economic education are comparable to those facing business enterprises and government institutions. They deal with such matters as allocating resources to achieve growth or efficiency, deciding whether long-run or short-run goals merit greatest attention, and determining standards and procedures for measuring the relative effectiveness of component parts. Economic educators also face conflicting value judgments involving social standards and responsibilities as they make decisions about where and how to bring about improvements in performance. For these reasons, making decisions about needed improvements and ways to bring them about will be an important and persistent problem.

8. How can we sustain support for economic education?

A comprehensive, clear response to this question involves considering, deciding, and dealing with such matters as these:

- Relative emphasis on volunteers and paid professionals.
- Relative emphasis on business, labor, agriculture, and government.
- Relative emphasis on state departments of education and collegiate institutions.
- Relative emphasis on public funds and private sources.
- Relative emphasis on professional educational organizations, corporate foundations, and private nonprofit education organizations.
- Relative emphasis on commercially published, privately sponsored, and government-produced teaching aids.

The need for choices related to how economic education should be supported is a persistent problem for social studies and economic educators. Since economic education does not as yet have an established place in the curriculum, there is a constant need not only to motivate and recruit financial supporters, but also to retain their interest and activity. This involves such matters as communications, participation, recognition, and the presentation of evidence to merit support. It also requires decisions about changes in sources of support which can result from changes in such factors as the economy, education generally, and the responsibilities of particular educational organizations. Problems related to the retention of support can emerge from both failures and successes in economic education and must be dealt with in terms of the sources of the problems. Problems related to control of the content of economic education can arise from the way financial support is generated. This area of concern will be persistent for administrators on the local level and for those committed to the economic education movement nationally.

PERSPECTIVES FOR DEALING WITH PERSISTENT ECONOMIC EDUCATION PROBLEMS

In addition to being aware of economic education problem areas, we must identify their major cause or causes. By doing this, one can discern the potentials for solving the problem, alleviating the problem, or being prepared to accept it as a persistent problem. In a field such as economic education, a measure of reassurance may come from discovering that many problems are produced by a success greater than anticipated, rather than by inadequacies in performance. This is exemplified by the problems associated with meeting the increased requests from school systems for assistance in improving their economic education programs. Such problems are real and may remain, but dealing with them can be more gratifying than taking corrective action due to failures. Based on the author's experiences, observations, and analysis, the following appear to be the major sources of problems. Remedial actions for each are implied and, if taken, can improve economic education; but they will not wholly eliminate the persistent problems discussed earlier.

1. Inadequate standards established
2. Inadequate guidance or supervision
3. Inadequate and/or misallocated funds
4. Unrealistic and/or ill-defined expectations
5. Inadequate and/or unqualified personnel
6. Changing needs
7. Competition for limited financial resources
8. Competition for limited available time
9. Inadequate coordination and/or communication
10. Inadequate public relations
11. Lack of leadership and/or assigned responsibility
12. Too many cooks
13. Inadequate research
14. Inadequate evaluation
15. Inadequate definition of aims
16. Inadequate tools
17. Inadequate follow-up

Another perspective provides reasons why social studies educators should have a positive outlook about the potentials for dealing with economic education problems. This observation is drawn by acknowledging the sound base that exists and the advances that have been made in economic education. At this stage of the economic education movement, such resources and developments as the following may be considered to be significant assets which can be capitalized upon:

1. Leadership of national coordinating organization
2. Widespread network of councils, centers, and cooperating school systems
3. Collegiate centers with specialized responsibilities and functions
4. Professionalization of economic education
5. Continuing concern about the economy and the field of economics
6. Market available for economic education in schools and communities
7. Tools and techniques available for economic education
8. Evidence of needs and successes available

Yet, even as we recognize the potential of such assets and the benefits of capitalizing upon them, we feel impelled to add another perspective from which to view the problems of economic education. Too often, we see teachers very lively and busy in their classrooms who remind us of people who climb trees but never stop to pick and eat the available fruit. They have to be helped to recognize that activities are fruitless, as far as economic education is concerned, unless the learning of economics takes place on the part of the students.

Another observation comes from being deluged with newsletters, catalogues, and checklists testifying to the abundant efforts to produce varied and more "hardware" and "software" for economic education. It would be useful for economic educators to bear in mind that a straight line is the shortest distance between two points, and that they should view critically any diversions which may involve waste of precious effort, time, and money for the basic teaching of economics. While we no longer seek only for the quality education epitomized picturesquely as having a great teacher such as Mark Hopkins on one end of a log and his student on the other, we should never underestimate the critical importance of the understanding, dedicated, competent teacher with or without aids and equipment.

SUMMARY

When one views the establishment, development, and nurturing of economic education as a process and the field of economic education as an institution, one can anticipate that problems will arise. Furthermore, experience will provide the basis for recognizing where problems are likely to emerge and which problem areas may persist.

What we recognize about the field of economic education is similar to what is recognized about such institutions as marriage and government. Those equipped to analyze the institutions can identify problem areas and, through guidance, can contribute to the improvement of individuals within the institution, as well as of the institution itself. This perspective shapes the agenda suggested for dealing with the persistent problems of economic education.

The task we are engaged in now in economic education, after thirty years of effort, is to prepare ourselves conscientiously and competently to serve the "market for economic education." Those entering the market have choices to make within problem areas, some of which they can recognize and others of which we shall do well to point out to them, based on our experiences. Choice-making within the field of economic education represents a test case for understanding the nature of scarcity and applying the fundamentals of economics to deal with it. We have to prepare ourselves to meet requests for guidance about the choices with responses appropriate to particular needs. Those responses have to be understood, so that the "purchasers of economic education" know what is being offered and what they are getting when they make their selections. Such competency and integrity on the part of the "sellers of economic education" will help to assure that our products will be accepted and used properly.

As we evaluate ourselves in terms of our success in dealing with problems, we can take pride in advances in the quantity of the product and amount of activity, but we must be cautious about basing judgment too heavily on those criteria. Where we have organizations, they should also be judged in terms of the appropriateness of their purposes, the adequacy of their personnel, the adequacy of their resources, and the time available to achieve their purposes. Where the teaching of economics takes place, it should also be judged in terms of consistency with purposes, comprehensiveness, and effectiveness. Where we have methods and materials being developed, they should also be judged in terms of consistency with purposes, usability by teachers, efficient expenditure of time and resources, and effectiveness. Where we have requirements established for teaching and learning economics, they should also be judged in terms of consistency with purposes, realism of resources available to meet the requirements, and validity of measuring their effectiveness. Where we receive support for economic education, it should also be judged as to whether it is provided consistent with our purposes, is under conditions acceptable to our standards and procedures, and includes our responsibility for being accountable to justify the support.

Looking ahead, we can anticipate that the major problem areas identified in this chapter will be persistent, but our increasingly valuable experiences and resources should enable us to provide responses of higher quality to the broad questions they pose. We should become even more aware of what should be included in defining the problems, more aware of the alternatives for choice and the consequences of the choices. Because of this, we should be more confident of the decisions we reach and more qualified to take effective action to advance economic education based on our conclusions. We can move outward to "larger rings" of knowledge and performance.

"Must" Reading in Economic Education for Social Studies Educators

S. STOWELL SYMMES

I t is perhaps presumptuous to select a reading list and then title it "must" reading, because there are many valuable curriculum items that are not reviewed here. There was, however, a conscious effort to keep the list short. In doing so, we have tried to emphasize titles which, when examined, would lead the reader to the many exciting student materials, research studies, curriculum bulletins, and philosophical articles in the field of economic education. Preparing massive lists of "Readings" without annotations is not only boring, but the result produces little incentive for exploration. It is hoped that these annotated selections will induce social studies educators to seek new vistas, to share their explorations with colleagues, and to become more effective participants in the process of economic education.

Readers are also urged to join the NCSS Economic and Consumer Education Special Interest Group (SIG). At a minimum, one member of every professional teaching staff should be designated as liaison to the NCSS Economic SIG and participate in its meetings. In this way, cross-discipline discussion will be fostered within social studies departments. Furthermore, with an economic education "specialist" on the staff of each school system, teaching technology in economics can be updated more effectively. School systems would do well to obtain a master set of the items reviewed below, and then place these materials in an accessible location under the supervision of an economic education specialist. Furthermore, social studies teachers should have access to the channels by which new developments in economic education will be disseminated. Links to the institutions responsible for curriculum change in economic education can be strengthened if social studies educators become familiar with the sources of information reviewed here.

American Enterprise Teaching Notes. New York: Playback Associates.

This complimentary newsletter features instructional economics activities at all grade levels. Edited by Helen Conover, *Teaching Notes* permits reproduction for classroom use. A wide range of teaching strategies has been covered in the eleven issues published to date. Back issues are available. Readers are given access to many different sources for instructional materials, and they will find that *Teaching Notes* serves as a forum for sharing ideas on how to teach economics effectively to students of varying age and ability levels. For back issues and mailing list status, write to: Playback Associates, 708 3rd Avenue, New York, New York 10017.

Checklist of Economic Education Materials for Teachers. New York: Joint Council on Economic Education. Published twice a year.

This is a free listing of all publications available through the Joint Council on Economic Education. Included are model curriculum guides, annotated bibliographies (games and simulations, audiovisual materials, children's stories), evaluation instruments, research studies, and general curriculum documents. Ask to be placed on the mailing list for *Update,* a quarterly newsletter. This will keep readers in contact with new programmatic developments in the field of economic education. Write to: Public Information Department, Joint Council on Economic Education, 1212 Avenue of the Americas, New York, New York 10036.

Consumer Education and Economic Education in the Public Schools, edited by Judith Staley Brenneke. New York: Joint Council on Economic Education, 1981.

Relationships between social studies education and consumer education are often strained. Some of the strain is due to lack of clear definitions of consumer education and failure to specify the linkages between consumer studies and economics. This publication is a report on a U.S. Department of Education-funded national conference held in 1980 to examine the connections between economics and consumer education. The papers and responses provide social studies educators with a philosophical base for integrating consumer content and economic content. One paper reviews nationally-normed economics tests, while another demonstrates how consumer economic content can be productively introduced through teaching units. Social studies teachers and teacher educators faced with state-mandated curriculums bearing on subjects related to economics will find that this book provides useful insights on how to meet such requirements within the context of adopted social studies objectives.

Directory of Social Studies/Social Science Service Organizations, by Frances Shilling Haley and Regina McCormick. Boulder, Colorado: ERIC/ChESS and Social Science Education Consortium, Inc., 1975.

Most of the professional service organizations listed in this valuable reference produce materials which can be helpful to economic educators. Detailed descriptions include statements of purpose, lists of publications, and types of service provided by 111 organizations covering every social science discipline and many related fields of study. All social studies teachers should have access to the membership privileges, particularly to the written materials made available by these organizations. A professional social science library should be established in every school system. The establishment of such a library can assure continuous institutional contact with the whole range of disciplines represented in this directory. Individual teachers cannot afford to join all, nor do they have sufficient interest in all. The social studies teaching staff, however, as a team, should have access to the marvelous resource base established by the organizations listed. The directory provides educators with addresses to expedite the formation of a first-rate social-science reference shelf at minimum cost. To order the directory, write to: Social Sciences Education Consortium, Inc., 855 Broadway, Boulder, Colorado 80302.

Economic Education Materials Catalog, by Norman Townshend-Zellner and Larry G. Little. San Diego: San Diego County Department of Education, 1978.

This catalog is a unique resource. It was designed to serve social studies teachers as a "clearinghouse" of exemplary economic education materials that could be used to implement the goals of California's *Social Sciences Education Curriculum Framework.* Materials in the catalog have been screened according to minimum criteria, which are published in the guide. Two-page information sheets describe the product features, explain how they can be used, give advice on economics background needed by students and teachers, identify concepts taught, specify how the material links to California's framework objectives, and explain how to obtain the material. For information about the catalog, contact: Economic Literacy Council of California, California State University & Colleges Foundation, Suite 218, 400 Golden Shore, Long Beach, California 90802.

Economics in Canadian Schools. Toronto, Canada: Canadian Foundation for Economic Education. Semiannual.

Readers of *Economics in Canadian Schools* will gain access to a wide range of well-written scholarly articles on various aspects of economics and economic instruction as seen through the eyes of our northern neighbors. This is a bilingual journal, which, in addition to outstanding articles, includes a book review section and a teacher-liaison column. Social studies educators in the United States would do well to become members of the Canadian Foundation for Economic Education. For a nominal fee, members receive single copies of all CFEE publications. These include the journal, *Rapport* (a bimonthly newsletter for teachers), "Issues in the Canadian Economy," publications in the "Understanding Economics" series, "Government and the Economy" series, and other instructional aids. Back issues of publications are available, some at no charge. For information, write to: Canadian Foundation for Economic Education, 252 Bloor Street, West, Suite S.560, Toronto, Ontario M5S 1V5 Canada.

Economics in Plain English, by Leonard Silk. New York: Simon and Schuster, 1978.

Social studies educators will find Leonard Silk's brief treatment of the economics discipline refreshing. The style of writing is conversational, with insightful references to historical events which dramatize the economic ideas under discussion. The author makes complex terminology come alive. He shows how mastering some basic tools of economic reasoning can increase the layperson's capacity to cope with the hard choices mandated by economic scarcity. The author introduces readers to a wide range of economic philosophies, both historical and current, without preaching a doctrine of his own. Furthermore, he examines the complex relationships between economic science and human values; and he shows that economics does connect the ordinary day-to-day tasks of living with the fundamental issues of all humankind. High school and college instructors of social studies can effectively use this book as a nontechnical supplementary text for students in courses on history, government, and sociology.

Educational Perspectives. Journal of the College of Education, University of Hawaii, Volume 17, Number 2, May 1978.

This issue features "selected aspects of economic education." It includes not only chapters which review current programs, but also some critiques of economic education materials and processes. Readers are treated to an overview of current economic education programs, a historical view of economic education in Hawaii, a description of economic education in Malaysia, an examination of concept learning as it relates to teacher behavior, and a view of materials development at the secondary level. Perhaps the most challenging chapters are "Five Perspectives of the Economic Education Curriculum" and "Economic Miseducation." These chapters analyze economic education orthodoxies in a thought-provoking manner.

List of Free Materials Available to Educators. Princeton, New Jersey: Prepared by The Educational Service Bureau, Dow Jones and Company, Inc. Updated annually.

This little reference book is one of the many excellent educational services provided by Dow Jones and Company. Listed are selections from about 100 diverse organizations, such as Federal Reserve Banks, the AFL-CIO, The Conference Board, the Chamber of Commerce of the United States, the American Institute of Cooperation, and the European Community Information Service. The organizations and their materials reflect a wide diversity of economic points of view. Having this booklet available gives teachers the addresses for many free materials which are useful in the classroom. To receive information about the activities of The Educational Service Bureau or about their Newspaper-in-Education Program, write to the nearest office: The Educational Service Bureau, Dow Jones and Company, Inc., P.O. Box 300, Princeton, New Jersey 08540; or 3525 Piedmont Rd., N.E., Six Piedmont Ctr., Suite 310, Atlanta, Georgia 30305; or 1701 Page Mill Road, Palo Alto, California 94304.

Master Curriculum Guide in Economics for the Nation's Schools, Part I, A Framework for Teaching Economics: Basic Concepts, W. Lee Hansen, G. L. Bach, James D. Calderwood and Phillip Saunders. New York: Joint Council on Economic Education, 1977.

This publication is designed to be used as a curriculum-planning document at the pre-college level. A rationale for economic literacy is presented, and the major elements of economic understanding are outlined. Concise overviews of the basic concepts considered essential tools for economic reasoning are given, and the reasoning process is illustrated through applied cases. A more detailed review and discussion of how this document can be useful to social studies educators may be found in the Social Science Education Consortium's Data Book, Boulder, Colorado, 1978.

Master Curriculum Guide in Economics for the Nation's Schools, Part II. New York: Joint Council on Economic Education.

Strategies for Teaching Economics Primary Level (grades 1–3), 1977
Strategies for Teaching Economics Intermediate Level (grades 4–6), 1978
Strategies for Teaching Basic and Consumer Education (secondary), 1979
Strategies for Teaching United States History (secondary), 1980
Strategies for Teaching World Studies (secondary), 1980
Strategies for Teaching Economics Junior High Level (grades 7–9), 1981

As a set, these six volumes are an excellent resource file of ready-to-use lessons which cut across grade levels and social studies courses. The strategies, organized around economic concepts treated in the Master Curriculum Guide *Framework,* are appropriate for infusion into ongoing social studies programs, and they can be adapted for learners of varying abilities.

Perspectives on Economic Education, edited by Donald R. Wentworth, W. Lee Hansen, and Sharryl H. Hawke. New York: Joint Council on Economic Education, Washington, D.C.: National Council for the Social Studies, and Boulder, Colorado: Social Science Education Consortium, Inc., 1977.

This book records the proceedings of the NSF-funded National Conference on Needed Research and Development in Pre-College Economic Education. The document contains an excellent review of the status of economic education in the 1970s, and it includes discussion papers on the fundamental problems of curriculum change which will confront social studies educators in the future. Chapter segments discuss economics as a discipline, economic education for ethnic minorities, teacher education both pre-service and in-service, student evaluation, and the delivery systems used by economic educators. Sixty specific recommendations for future research and program development are presented.

Research in Economic Education Report Number 2, *Attitudes and Opinions on Economic Issues,* by George G. Dawson. Old Westbury, New York: Empire State College, 1980.

This publication illustrates the wide body of research that is available in the field of economic education. Readers will become aware of the *Journal of Economic Education* and other valuable sources of research data on the teaching-learning process in the field of economic education. In Report Number 2, Dawson summarizes scores of published research studies in the controversial field of economic opinions, an area of study which should be of special interest to social studies educators. He has prepared a masterful introduction that examines the problems of opinion and attitude research. The document also contains reproductions of several examples of attitude/opinion instruments that researchers have used to gather data. To acquire copies of this publication and to obtain assistance related to economic education research topics, contact George Dawson, Director, Center for Economic Education, Empire State College, Long Island Regional Learning Center, State University of New York, Old Westbury, New York 11568.

"Revision of the Social Studies Curriculum Guidelines," *Social Education,* April 1979, pp. 261-273. Washington, D.C.: National Council for the Social Studies.

Many excellent *Social Education* articles on economics-related subjects could be annotated here, but space will not permit such treatment. Readers are urged to consult back issues of the journal and to use the indices published in the November/December issues each year as a means of locating relevant articles. Social studies educators know that the guidelines for their discipline that were published in April 1979 are not carved in stone. Revisions and updates will be required periodically. It is useful, however, to examine the current guidelines after reading this Bulletin. Doing so will underscore the mutuality of interests shared by economic educators and social studies educators.

Selective Bibliography in Economics Resources, by Judith E. Headstrom. Boulder Colorado: Social Science Education Consortium, Inc., and ERIC/ChESS, 1977.

The value of this publication lies in having annotations of a wide range of materials, including textbooks, teacher's guides, simulations, audiovisuals, and supplementary print materials. The primary focus is on teaching and learning economics as a social science discipline, but some materials dealing with personal and consumer economics are included.

Skill Development in the K-6 Social Studies Program. Bulletin No. 5193. Madison, Wisconsin: Wisconsin Department of Public Instruction, 1979.

This document is a good example of an effort to delineate a skills matrix across grade levels. Although the Bulletin does not refer specifically to economic content, the approach to skill development which is used can easily be adapted to the needs of economic education. As stated in the introduction, "skills and competencies provide students with the tools to make better sense out of their social environments so as to become better decision-makers." The publication also will be helpful to those readers interested in projecting thinking processes into the secondary social studies classes. For more information, resources, bibliographies, and assistance on skill development, contact: H. Michael Hartoonian, Social Studies Specialist, Wisconsin Department of Public Instruction, 125 South Webster Street, P.O. Box 7841, Madison, Wisconsin 53707.

Social Science Record, Journal of the New York State Council for the Social Studies, Volume XVII, No. 2, Winter 1980.

This special issue of the NYSCSS journal features a series of articles on integrating economics into the social studies. In addition to finding general information, readers will discover some exciting chapters on practical classroom teaching, such as "Meeting the Needs of Non-Academic Low Income Students and Their Parents in the 1980's"; "Integrating Economics into the Study of India"; and "How to Establish a 'Private' Economy in the Elementary Classroom." For back issues and subscription information, contact: William Elwell, Department of Curriculum and Instruction, State University College, Brockport, New York 14420.

Strategies for Teaching Economics via Social Studies Methods K-12. New York: Joint Council on Economic Education. Expected publication date: fall 1981.

This publication will be an edited version of a document prepared by professors of social studies under the direction of Dennis Weidenaar at Purdue University. A summer seminar designed to introduce university professors of social studies to the economics discipline resulted in this unique publication, which blends economic concept development with classroom methodology. Economic instructional techniques are used to illustrate concept development, inquiry, skills learning, and valuing. Social studies teacher educators and economic education workshop directors will find the lessons especially relevant.

Teacher's Guide for the Basic Competencies in Reasoning. Montpelier, Vermont: Vermont Department of Education, 1979.

This booklet can be used by social science teachers at all grade levels, not only to explore the component parts of reasoning, but also to teach specific thinking skills. The authors tried to synthesize elements common to most models of inquiry and critical thinking. Those skills selected fit the objectives of economic education very well: Problem Solving, Classifying and Organizing, Making Reasoned Judgments, and Research Skills. The guide includes sample teaching strategies and mastery level examples for each competency. Readers are given sufficient numbers of concrete techniques to enable them to generate their own exercises linked closely to the subject areas at hand. Reasoning skills can be effectively practiced in the context of economic problem analysis. For information on the guide, contact: James Lengel, Social Studies Consultant, Division of Elementary and Secondary Education, State of Vermont Department of Education, Montpelier, Vermont 05602.

Teaching Activities in Economics. University of Missouri, Columbia: Missouri Council on Economic Education and the Center for Economic Education, 1976–77.

This publication is one of several hundred economic education curriculum documents produced and distributed by the Joint Council on Economic Education's network of affiliated Councils and university Centers. A free *Directory* of affiliates and, upon request, a listing of materials produced and distributed by the network are available from the JCEE. (See address under *Checklist.*) *Teaching Activities in Economics* was selected for annotation here because it symbolizes the functional services of the state Councils and university Centers for Economic Education. The publication contains teaching plans developed by elementary and secondary teachers who attended summer workshops at the University of Missouri-Columbia. The lessons were selected for publication, edited and revised to fit a standard format, and then keyed to the social studies objectives of the Basic Essential Skills Test which is given to all eighth graders by the Missouri Deparment of Elementary and Secondary Education. Objectives are specified for primary, intermediate, and junior high levels, and they are also cross-referenced to the classroom activities. To obtain copies at $5.00 per copy, write to: Missouri Council on Economic Education, 9 Middlebush Hall, University of Missouri-Columbia, Columbia, Missouri 65211.

Teaching High School Economics, Fourth Edition, by Edward C. Prehn. New York: New York City Council on Economic Education, 1981.

This highly readable work is filled with common-sense advice on teaching economics. Discussions of learning theory are punctuated with illustrative lesson plans. Step-by-step tips on organizing student activities, such as field trips and classroom simulations, are interspersed with practical aids to more effective lesson-plan development. Chapters are devoted to making economics relevant for inner-city students; and advice is provided on teaching slow learners, in addition to teaching about urban economic problems, environmental problems, and global economic issues. Edward Prehn has included a listing of books and materials which he recommends as a basic economic education library for social studies teachers.

Teaching With Case Studies, by Paul H. Tedesco. Boston, Massachusetts: Public Information Center, Federal Reserve Bank of Boston, 1974.

This little book is an excellent resource guide, especially for teachers interested in developing their own materials to supplement textbook lessons. The methodology for using case studies, featuring a section on the art of asking questions which will elicit problem-solving thought processes, is clearly delineated. The book contains a straightforward presentation on how to collect case materials that will help social studies teachers mine the varied sources of information available at the local level. Paul Tedesco is also responsible for coordinating the Business and Economic Life Program (BHELP) at Northeastern University. Teachers can benefit from reading the BHELP Newsletter on a regular basis. Write to: Business History and Economic Life Program, Inc., 219 CU, College of Education, Northeastern University, Boston, MA 02115

The Elementary Economist. Cambridge, Massachusetts: The National Center of Economic Education for Children.

The Elementary Economist is a free newsletter that features curriculum strategies devoted to teaching economic ideas from K to 6. Permission to reproduce published lessons is given. Readers will find numerous examples of lessons which meet the objectives of their state or schoolwide social studies programs. For copies and mailing list status, write to: Lesley College, Cambridge, Massachusetts 02238.

The Indiana Social Studies Quarterly, Official organ of the Indiana Council for the Social Studies. Muncie, Indiana: Ball State University. Volume XXV, No. 3, Winter, 1972-73.

Although this special issue, entitled "Understanding and Teaching Economics," is nearly ten years old, readers will find some excellent substantive chapters of more than historical interest. A chapter on "Institutionalizing the Process of Curriculum Change: An Indiana Experiment" provides a case study of the way one state has organized to implement economic education. Other chapters express clear rationales for economic instruction at all grade levels. Many of these statements have stood the test of time and can be used in the 1980s by social studies educators to justify linkages to economic education.

The Study and Teaching of Economics, by Roman F. Warmke, Raymond H. Muessig, and Steve L. Miller. Columbus, Ohio: Charles E. Merrill Publishing Company, 1980.

This is one of six books in Merrill's *The Study and Teaching of Social Science Series,* each dealing with a separate discipline. The authors have combined to create a professional reference that clearly and concisely delineates the "kit of tools" used by economists. Economic ideas are presented as exciting and dynamic tools useful for participation in economic life as consumers, producers, workers, and citizen-voters. Technical terminology is explained in understandable language which avoids "jargon." Teachers will appreciate the excellent index, which makes it easy to locate concept clusters. The chapter on "Suggested Methods for Teachers" provides wonderfully fresh approaches to teaching the "dismal" science. In addition to discussing traditional materials, the authors describe creative ways to use bumper stickers, poems, newspapers, children's books, simulations, and rock music to engage students in learning about economics.

Trade-offs: What the Research Is Saying, Research Report Number 82, 1980. Bloomington, Indiana: Agency for Instructional Television.

This paper reviews 15 different studies that have examined the impact of *Trade-offs,* a television series designed to improve and expand economics instruction in fifth- and sixth-grade classrooms. Social studies teachers will find the 18-page report of interest not only because it critiques economic education research methodologies, but also because it provides evidence to support the contention that economic instruction can be productively introduced at intermediate and middle-school grade levels. Students' knowledge about and attitudes toward economics are found to be significantly improved by using *Trade-offs.* The report also concludes that in-service education in economics improves teacher attitudes toward the discipline. Available from AIT, Box A, Bloomington, IN 47401.

Wingspread Workbook for Educational Change Agents, by James M. Becker and Carole L. Hahn. Boulder, Colorado: Social Science Education Consortium, Inc., 1975.

This workbook is not designed specifically for economic educators, but the techniques presented can be usefully applied by social studies teachers who wish to make an impact on the economic component of their curricula. It is an appropriate guide for looking at how curriculum leaders (change agents) can help a school system adopt "innovations." The authors define innovations as those ideas, techniques, and products that are perceived as being new. The *Wingspread Workbook* procedures may work best when applied to adopting new curriculum materials, but readers interested in changing ideas can also gain from the discussion of diffusion theory and from the references given.

INDEX

Anita Draper, Indexer